*"I looked down at Roy with something akin to awe. He had grown and
filled out and his coat, no longer yellow but a rich gold, lay in luxuriant shining
swaths over the well-fleshed ribs and back. A new, brightly studded collar glittered on
his neck and his tail, beautifully fringed, fanned the air gently. He was now a Golden
Retriever in full magnificence. As I stared at him he reared up, plunked his fore paws on
my chest and looked me in the face, and in his eyes I read plainly . . . calm affection and trust. . . ."*
—James Herriot, "Mrs. Donovan" in *James Herriot's Dog Stories*, 1986

Goldens Forever

A Heartwarming Celebration of the Golden Retriever

Todd R. Berger, Editor

With stories by Sam Savitt, Gary Shiebler, Muriel Dobbin, Joseph Monninger, Ann Raincock, Charles Kulander, and others

Voyageur Press

PetLife
LIBRARY

Paperback edition first published in 2006 by Voyageur Press, an imprint of MBI Publishing Company, Galtier Plaza, Suite 200, 380 Jackson Street, St. Paul, MN 55101-3885 USA

MBI Publishing Company titles are also available at discounts in bulk quantity for industrial or sales-promotional use. For details write to Special Sales Manager at MBI Publishing Company, Galtier Plaza, Suite 200, 380 Jackson Street, St. Paul, MN 55101-3885 USA

ISBN-13: 978-0-7603-2899-6
ISBN-10: 0-7603-2899-4

Editor: Todd R. Berger
Designer: Kjerstin Moody

Printed in Hong Kong

Credits:
On the cover: Photograph © Henry H. Holdsworth/Wild by Nature

On the back cover: Photographs © Henry H. Holdsworth/Wild by Nature

Contents

Introduction

A golden retriever looked up at me today as I made breakfast in my second-floor apartment. From my kitchen window, I was greeted by the kind, dark-brown eyes and sweeping tail of my neighbors' golden, sitting on the deck behind their house. I put some bagels in the toaster oven, and I sipped orange juice, temporarily distracted by gastro-intestinal needs. But when I looked down again toward the deck, he was still watching me. On some mornings, he barks at me a couple of times when I look down, adding a little emphasis to his greeting. On others, like today, he sits there quietly, watching me. Finishing my breakfast, I stepped away from the window to get ready for work. When I came back through the kitchen on my way out the door, I looked down again, as I always do, to see if he is there. But his owner had brought him inside, and it was time for me to go. I picked up my bag, stepped out the door, and drove away, knowing he will be there tomorrow morning, watching me, with kind, dark-brown eyes and a sweeping tail.

I am hardly the first, or the only, person to be captivated by a golden retriever. Around the world, hundreds of thousands of happy golden owners, as well as millions more who happen to encounter a golden retriever while going about their day, have been swept up by the charms of the breed.

Though most of these goldens are snoozing away on the sofas of not-so-well-known families, some goldens lounge around the living rooms of people with household names. Among the famous who have succumbed at one time or another to the golden's allure are actress Mary Tyler Moore, *60 Minutes* correspondent Morley Safer, actor Jimmy Stewart, Los Angeles Lakers basketball coach Phil Jackson, singer Jimmy Buffet, actor Gregory Peck, *Today* show host Matt Lauer, syndicated columnist and author Dave Barry, and actress Renee Zellweger.

Sometimes the golden retriever's almost mystical power over people results in some down-right bizarre events. In 1993, the town of Guffey, Colorado, elected a golden retriever named Shanda mayor. Former President Gerald Ford sometimes took his golden retriever Liberty snowmobiling and once got locked out of the White House while taking Liberty for a walk. Alex, the golden retriever that appeared in Stroh's beer commercials in the United States in the 1990s, fetched and opened beers for his master.

Most owners of a golden retriever, however, don't see their dog rise to high political office, socialize with presidents and kings, or become famous for popping open brewskies on national television. So what is it, then, that brings so many into the golden retriever fold? Surely some of the lure lies in the golden's gentle nature, eagerness to please his owner (or whoever stops to pet him), intelligence, willingness to help her owner in any way needed, and talent as a gun dog. Probably even more reasons lie in the breed's kindly eyes, beautiful feathered coat, and face that appears to be grinning at you at all times. Perhaps it is all of these things, combined in some super-secret way, that renders humanity helpless at the paws of the golden retriever.

Snoozing in the back of a pick-up truck. Photograph © Lon E. Lauber

The tall green grass of Wyoming's Teton Valley nearly swallows this golden. Photograph © Henry H. Holdsworth/ Wild by Nature

About *Goldens Forever*

Goldens Forever is the second anthology spotlighting golden retrievers in Voyageur Press's PetLife Library, following in the footsteps of the bestseller *Love of Goldens* (1998). *Goldens Forever* focuses on the hallmarks of the golden retriever: their endearing nature, intelligence, and ability and desire to aid people in need. Including the work of the best writers, photographers, and artists of the last twenty-five years who turned their attention to golden retrievers, *Goldens Forever* is filled with beautiful images of and elegant prose about a remarkable breed.

It is time for our first story. However, it is strongly recommended that you turn the page only in the company of kind, dark-brown eyes and a sweeping tail.

"Ready to Go" by Robert K. Abbett. From the original oil painting. Reprinted by permission of the artist.

Part I:
A Friendly Furball

"As he [our golden retriever Ben] became acquainted, he never barked at a neighbor, but strangers were announced loudly. He became everybody's dog. Even dog-indifferent people found being welcomed by this merry heart irresistible."
Ruth Gordon, *Magic Dog,* 1995

Left: *With head curiously cocked, a golden pauses in an autumn field. Photograph © Henry H. Holdsworth/Wild by Nature*
Above: *A whole pack of friendly furballs naps in a golden pile. Photograph © Henry H. Holdsworth/Wild by Nature*

Randy

by Sam Savitt

Golden owners near and far have thrilled to come home to a friendly furball, a golden retriever almost beside himself to see his family return. The golden's amicable nature also draws people in, strangers attracted to the beautiful dog with the friend-to-all temperament. It is not hard to see why the golden retriever is one of the most popular family pets in the world.

Though he started out as an artist, Sam Savitt eventually turned his pen to writing about the endearing nature of the golden retriever, among other topics. As he told *Contemporary Authors* in the mid-1980s: "Sometimes I find it easier to 'say dog than to draw dog' and I write to take a break from the problems of color, tone, value and getting a three-dimensional effect on a flat surface." He has written more than twenty books, including *Midnight, Champion Bucking Horse* (1958); *Day at the L.B.J. Ranch* (1965); *Ups and Downs* (1973); and *A Horse to Remember* (1984). He has also illustrated more than one hundred books, including many of the titles he authored.

"Randy" first appeared in Savitt's *The Dingle Ridge Fox and Other Stories* (1978), a wonderful collection of animal tales.

The kind and patient nature of the golden is renowned, and these traits that so endear the breed to human-kind are evident in the youngest of yellow-locked pups. Photograph © Henry H. Holdsworth/Wild by Nature

JON RADCLIFF HAD always owned golden retrievers, and when his old dog died, he purchased another of the same breed. Although he never exhibited his dogs, he always bought the caliber of the breed that would "show." His newly acquired six-month-old puppy promised to be as handsome as any of the others.

The home the puppy was brought to was a magnificent white manor house on a high hill. It stood regally in the midst of rolling velvet lawns and flower beds that were just beginning to come awake in the early spring sunshine.

Mr. Radcliff called the new arrival Randy, the same name he had given to all his other dogs. After the puppy was housebroken by the butler, he was allowed the run of the house. It was a spacious place with many carpeted rooms and an abundance of armchairs and couches—the dream of any energetic, mischievous puppy.

It was an adult home Randy had come to, and a rather cold one. Mrs. Radcliff openly disliked dogs, and Mr. Radcliff's interest in them was one of possession rather than love. Randy sensed this and avoided them both, but he got along well with everyone else. Annie, the cook, usually had a delectable tidbit for him, and the chauffeur always had a kind word. But the puppy had little real companionship. The only member of the household who played with him occasionally was Mr. Brenner, the old gardener, who also scolded whenever he found him digging in the flower beds.

By October, Randy had become a truly beautiful golden retriever. He had settled down quite a bit. Now that he was a year old, he wore a leather collar with his name engraved on the brass plate affixed to it.

Randy was a loner who sat on the front lawn a good part of the day watching an occasional car or a horseback rider go by. He sometimes trotted down the long graveled driveway to the dirt road to stand at its edge, gazing off into the distance. But he never roamed away from the house.

He was a quiet, good-natured dog, seemingly happy and contented. His first winter with the Radcliffs was spent mostly indoors or down below the house where he could survey the frozen pond and the neighborhood children skating on the far side.

But in early April, when the green began filtering up through the brown fields, the golden-coated dog became restless, and soon he was spending more time in the surrounding countryside than on his front lawn. Often when he did not show up for dinner, his owner dispatched the chauffeur to look for him. The man usually found him wandering aimlessly along one of the many roads that crisscrossed the area. When the chauffeur called, Randy obediently got into the limousine and rode home sitting quietly in the back seat.

As spring became summer, Randy drifted further away from the Radcliff house. Sometimes when he returned after being absent for a day or two his owner locked him in the kennel for a while, hoping this might dampen his wanderlust. But the moment the dog was released, he was off again.

The countryside was spotted with farms and groups of small houses.

A mucky golden in a northern marsh.
Photograph © Bill Marchel

Randy got to know the residents and before long most of them became familiar with the handsome golden retriever whose warm, friendly manner charmed all who met him.

"Hi, Randy!" the children would cry as he came trotting up to them. He accepted their welcome with a great show of tail wagging, grinning broadly as small hands reached out to him. He was never pushy or overbearing, and when he had had enough, he moved on up the road.

When he met strange dogs, he stood his ground in a manner that was neither aggressive nor defensive and none ever tried to stand in his way.

The golden dog stopped in occasionally to visit the Radcliffs, who had just about given up on him. Mr. Radcliff, however, was still hopeful that one day Randy would get over his roving ways and come back to stay.

But Randy was his own dog now. He made no attachments. He had become a drifter, an amiable tramp. Yet, anyone watching the purposeful way he trotted across the fields or up the middle of a road might feel that here was a dog in search of something.

The Lucas farm lay in a small valley about two miles away from the Radcliff residence. It was owned and operated by young Warren Lucas, who took great pride in his fine milch cows and immaculately kept cowbarn and outbuildings.

One morning in the middle of July, Randy stopped at the gate where

Gentleness of the soul is mirrored in the eyes. Photograph © Henry H. Holdsworth/Wild by Nature

the two Lucas children were playing quietly in the driveway in front of the low white farm house. Behind them a number of geese and white ducks quacked in the barnyard. On the far hillside beyond, a scattering of sheep grazed peacefully. In the adjoining meadows, black-and-white spotted cows rested in dark groups in the shade of the willow trees.

Perhaps the complete tranquillity of the scene held the dog there. For a moment he seemed unable to make up his mind whether to go on or join the children. Then suddenly, waving his golden plume aloft, he bounded up to the little boy and girl. He seemed to be grinning from ear to ear, as if to say, "Here I am. Aren't you lucky I've come to visit you!"

The visit became a stay. The children fell in love with their new pet immediately, and it certainly looked as if Randy had no intention of leaving. Warren Lucas checked with some of his neighbors about the dog's identity. They all remembered seeing him around but the brass plate on his collar only said that his name was Randy, nothing else.

The Radcliff chauffeur spotted the golden retriever on the Lucas front lawn a short time later. He recognized the dog instantly and brought him home. Two days later Randy was back with the Lucases. The chauffeur picked him up again, and Randy returned to the Lucas family again.

This back-and-forth game went on through the month of August. At times, Randy returned to the Lucas farm every day. More often, two or three days elapsed before he made it back.

One evening in the beginning of September, Mr. Radcliff phoned Warren Lucas.

"Look here, sir," he announced. His voice was more annoyed than angry. "My chauffeur has picked up my dog at your place over twenty times this past month. That's getting a bit ridiculous, don't you think?"

"I'm sorry about that," the farmer replied, "but what can I do about it?"

"Not much, I suppose," Mr. Radcliff answered, "but I think that the best thing for me to do at this point is give him to you!"

Warren Lucas and his comely, red-haired wife, Betty, were delighted to accept this beautiful gift, and of course the children were overjoyed. Randy was now officially theirs, and for a while it seemed that the golden retriever had found what he was looking for at last.

The Lucas dairy farm had everything that Randy loved—cows, pigs, sheep, chickens, geese, and flocks of doves that zoomed constantly over the barnyard or lined up like white banners along the crest of the barn roof. In the mornings the dog joined his new owner in the cowshed while the milking machines were in action.

The young farmer became extremely fond of Randy, as he could not help but respond to the retriever's friendliness. And although the dog still romped with the children after school, he seemed to have become their father's companion. He followed the farmer about as he did his chores and frequently rode beside him in the cab of the pickup truck. But Warren Lucas knew dogs and he recognized in this one a certain independence and a touch of aloofness that somehow kept them apart.

The snow came early in December, banking against the farm buildings and blocking the driveways. Randy began to trail along behind the tractor as Warren Lucas pushed the drifts aside. In the winter evenings, Betty Lucas would prepare Randy's dinner, and afterward the dog would stretch out before the fireplace, perhaps dreaming of the places he'd been or of adventures yet to come.

The "January thaw" came in the second week of February. The mud was knee deep for three days; then winter seemed to start all over again. March blew in with a tremendous snowstorm and the drifts did not begin to melt until the end of the month.

Then, one morning in early April, Randy walked out the driveway and turned east.

Warren Lucas saw him leave. He called out, "Hey, Randy, come back!" But Randy was on his way.

That evening the children asked where the dog had gone.

Their father stood by the window gazing in the direction Randy had taken. All that afternoon he had been watching, hoping against hope. He smiled sadly at the youngsters.

"Randy has got spring fever," he said as he filled his pipe. "He has the urge to travel on—maybe he'll come back."

But in his heart he knew that Randy never would.

All through the following summer Randy shifted from one place to the next, covering an area of approximately twenty square miles. He rarely went hungry, as most people were pleased to give him food when he came to the door. How could they resist the charming individual with the golden coat? Some tried to entice him to stay on, but to no avail.

Actually, Randy was a strange dog—outgoing, affable, but still basically a loner. He did not join any of the dogs that roamed about and never ran deer or other wild game. He was constantly on the move—seemingly lighthearted yet somehow haunted by some obscure force that pushed him ever onward, allowing him no time to settle down or take root anywhere.

On an afternoon in September, Randy was proceeding north along the shoulder of a hardtop road just south of the county line.

The day was extremely hot and humid for September. Randy was thirsty and, to add to his discomfort, police cars began appearing, driving slowly past him, going in both directions. Automobiles never bothered Randy. Right from the beginning of his travels he had learned to keep out of their way. But these cars had speakers that blared loudly and abrasively. Finally, ears tucked back, he turned off the road into the woods. He met an old cowpath and followed it downhill to a narrow strip of marshland. Here he lay in a shallow stream for a little while, lapping the water and feeling the wet coolness against his belly. Later he got up, shook himself, and wandered across a brush-covered field to an abandoned apple orchard on the far side. Now he could no longer hear the loudspeakers. Up ahead beyond the orchard the woods became almost impenetrable with windfalls and tangles of vines. Randy skirted them, then swung upgrade to pick up the road once more where the going would be easier.

A whimpering sound stopped him in his tracks. With lowered head,

Late summer sunshine warms a handsome golden. Photograph © William H. Mullins

The Tale of Fox Tail

by Victor H. Austin, D.V.M.

One day, a beautiful, healthy-looking male golden retriever appeared at the closed glass front door of the veterinary hospital in Ventura, California. The doctor I was working for was not in the office at that time, and I questioned the receptionist as to what the dog was doing. She hadn't noticed him until I asked the question, but she immediately replied, "Open the door and let Fred in."

Fred walked in when I opened the door, walked to the nearest vacant exam room, placed his front paws on the exam table, and waited to be lifted up, which the attendant did. Fred positioned himself on the table (head end towards the hanging otoscope) and tilted his head to the side. Joe said, "Look in his ear." He steadied Fred's head while I looked in and saw a large, fresh foxtail awn, something common with many open lots and no leash laws. I immediately removed it.

Fred jumped to the floor, went to the front door, and waited for Joe to open it. He looked like he was smiling as he trotted out the door and down the street toward home. Jennie, the receptionist, picked up the phone and called the dog's owner, Mrs. Taylor. "Fred was just here—the foxtail was in his right ear. Watch for any trouble." Mrs. Taylor thanked her and said, "Bill us, as usual."

Dr. Victor H. Austin is a California-based veterinarian.

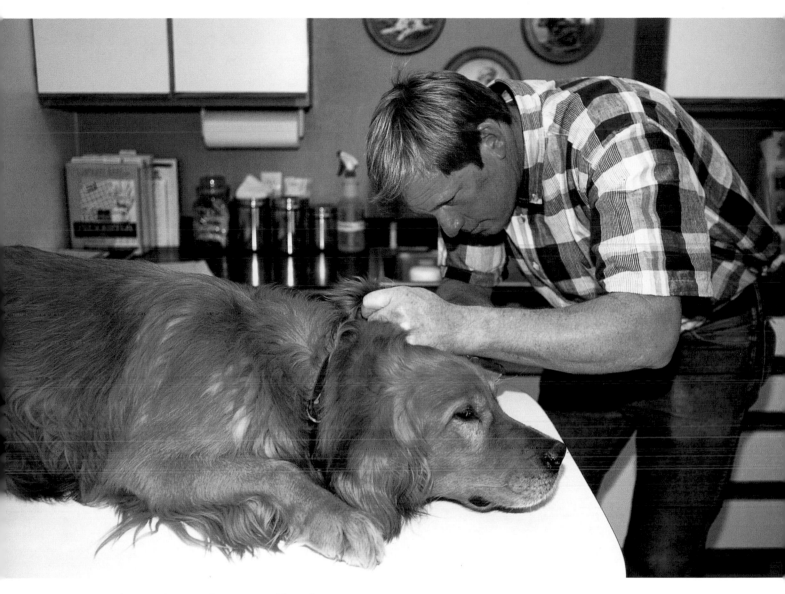

A trip to the vet. Photograph © Bill Buckley/The Green Agency

he stalked cautiously forward to investigate and suddenly came face to face with a small boy. The child was standing alone in a mass of green ferns. His blond hair was plastered against his forehead and tear-stained cheeks. His blue shirt, ripped by thorns, hung limply against his small body.

Wiggling upside-down through the snow, a golden eyeballs her owner. Photograph © Henry H. Holdsworth/Wild by Nature

The four-year-old had been lost in the woods since early that morning when he had wandered away from his home to pick berries.

The police loudspeakers had been calling him: "Billy, come to the road! Billy, come to the road!" But Billy could not hear them, and even if he had, he would not have known where the road was.

To Randy, the youngster was no different from the many other children he had met. And Randy's wagging tail and grinning face told Billy this was a friend.

A friend was what Billy needed now more than anything in the world. His little hands reached out to clutch the leather collar, and Randy started off in the direction he had been going. Because he was a "gentleman" and in no hurry, he walked slowly to allow the boy to keep up. At one time the child stumbled and let go. Randy stopped and waited for him to rise and take hold once more.

After almost an hour, the pair emerged from the woods onto the road. Minutes later a patrol car pulled up alongside them. A policeman got out and picked up the child. He held the back door open for Randy, who leaped in without a moment's hesitation. He had ridden in a limousine at one time, and a pickup truck not too long ago. As far as he was concerned, a patrol car was no different.

They arrived in front of a small farmhouse a short time later. There were other automobiles parked in the driveway near several people. Billy's mother came rushing to the police car when she saw her son in the front seat beside the officer. She wept with joy when she held the child in her arms.

"Oh, you found him! You found him!" she cried over and over again.

The officer smiled.

"It wasn't me that found your boy, ma'am," he declared. "It was this dog that did it!"

He pointed to Randy. "Saw them both come out of the woods together, the dog leading and the boy hanging on."

Of course Randy became an instant hero. He did not know what great feat he had accomplished, but he was not one to question the praise and adoration he was suddenly receiving.

With a tongue longer than the desired Popsicle itself, a golden slathers his tongue all over a lemon-lime treat on a hot summer day. Photograph © J. Hatten Photo Illustrations

All four paws airborne, a golden sprints along a rocky lakeshore. Photograph © William H. Mullins

He was invited into Billy Armor's home and given an enormous meal, the like of which he had not had in a long time. That evening a reporter came to the house with notebook and camera, and the following weekend a picture of Billy and Randy appeared in the local newspaper with the story of how this wonderful dog had rescued the lost child.

Randy lived with the Armors for more than two weeks. Mrs. Armor wanted to keep him but felt it her duty to find out who owned this treasure. She made constant inquiries and ran an ad in the lost-and-found section of the newspaper, but there were no answers.

She groomed the dog every day until his coat took on an added golden luster. The family would have been delighted if Randy had chosen to live with them forever but, one cool afternoon in the beginning of October, Randy hit the trail once more.

All that morning he had been sitting in front of the Armors' house with his nose lifted to the wind. Huge swirls of blowing leaves whipped across the grass and heaped against the front porch in fluttering mounds of yellow and red. Just after noon, Randy meandered out the open gate of the front yard and turned south along the same road he had been following north just a few weeks earlier.

High overhead a formation of Canada geese preceded him. The sky was overcast, with the sun breaking through occasionally to splash its brightness across the land.

Randy quickened his pace as the faint honking notes of the migrating birds reached him, urging him on.

Katie Conklin lived in a dilapidated brown house along one of the many dirt roads that wound its way through the center of the county. She was a small woman, thin and slightly bent. There was an allover gray look about her—shoes, faded print dress, hair. But her eyes, deep set and dark, belied the drabness of her appearance.

She had been born in this house. It had been a working farm then. The barn had been occupied by a team of Clydesdales and many cows, and the summer fields had been green with corn. She had especially loved the time of haying and late August when vegetables and fruits were put up for the winter. But after her husband was killed in a tractor accident, the farm deteriorated rapidly, for they had no children to carry on. Katie continued to live there with an older sister. The two women could sometimes be seen walking slowly together down to an isolated country store where they did their shopping.

After her sister died, Katie was rarely seen outdoors again. She survived on a small income that had been left to her in a family will, and the only one who ever looked in on the old woman was an elderly man who came up from the store to bring her food.

Katie had become a recluse. She was completely alone. Day after day she sat by her kitchen window and stared out at the changing seasons. Now it was early autumn. The days were still warm, but lately in the morning there was frost in the long valley below the house.

For the past week Katie had been aware that a beautiful, golden-colored dog was in the area. Once she had seen it go by on the road, and just the day before she had noticed him, moving along the fence line behind the barn.

He made her think of a small brown dog she had had when she was a child—it seemed so long ago. Way back in the recesses of her memory she could almost see him—leaping, barking with joy whenever they met.

All the following morning Katie sat on her porch hoping to see the golden dog again. He did not appear that day or the next, but on the afternoon of the third day she saw him from her bedroom window—this time trotting up the road, heading in the direction of her house.

Katie quickly wrapped a shawl around her shoulders and hurried down the porch steps to the edge of the road.

As Randy came along, she stooped forward and reached out her hand.

"Hey, big dog," she called softly.

Randy turned toward her and stopped just beyond her reach. In the past he had only been approached like this by children. He seemed suspicious for a moment, but because he had such a good-natured, friendly character he walked up to the gray-haired woman and allowed her fingers to stroke the top of his head gently.

Katie's hand touched his collar. She turned her head to one side and squinted her eyes so that she could read the brass plate more easily. She rubbed its surface with her thumb to clear off the grime it had accumulated.

"My, you have a beautiful name," she breathed. "A long time ago," she revealed, smiling, "I had a dog like you—not as pretty perhaps, but he was a nice dog and I loved him very much."

Tears welled into her eyes. "I remember now," she went on. "I called him Willy—strange that I should forget such a simple name."

Randy did not understand a word she was saying but something held him there. He closed his eyes, panting softly, as Katie's gentle hand caressed the thick fur of his shiny coat.

"How would you like to come in for a drink of water?" she asked. "You look warm."

The old woman straightened up and turned back to her house.

Randy remained standing where he was. He seemed puzzled—and uncertain. Then he followed her up the porch steps and sat back on his haunches facing the door.

Katie went inside and quickly returned with a bowl of cool water. She placed it on the floor in front of him. The dog was not thirsty but he took a few courteous laps.

Afterward he returned to the road and continued on his way. He looked back once to see Katie still on the porch, her pale face turned toward him, her hand raised to shield her eyes from the sun just going down behind the trees.

Randy returned two days later. Since he had left Katie Conklin, he had been wandering through the countryside. But instead of moving on, an unexplainable compulsion seemed to draw him back to the old woman.

Gray-muzzled and sleepy, a senior citizen golden nods off on a backyard deck. Photograph © Sharon Eide/Elizabeth Flynn

He approached Katie's house from the field behind it late in the day. The sun had already set, but a pink afterglow remained. It was the hour of silhouettes when the distant hills become deep purple and the trees are etched in black against the sky.

A faint yellow light appeared in one of the windows as Randy came up to the back porch and lay down. The evening was warm and soon the air was alive with the sounds of the forest.

The door suddenly opened and Katie came out. She seated herself in a rocking chair, then discerned Randy in the gloom below her.

She was not startled. It was almost as if she expected him to be there.

"Good evening, Randy," she said quietly. "Why don't you come up and sit here beside me?"

She held out her hand and Randy came up to it, ducking his head slightly so that her fingers could reach the soft fur of his neck. They sat there together until the evening deepened into night and the stars glittered overhead.

The old woman had given up. She had turned inward. She had separated herself from the outside world and had allowed her utter loneliness and despair to take over. Now for the first time in years she was conscious of a new warmth within her and a wondrous feeling of peace and contentment.

Katie opened her eyes. She had fallen asleep, but the chill night air awakened her. The golden dog was no longer there. She peered into the darkness and called his name, then finally rose to her feet and walked slowly back into the house.

The following night Randy came by again. It had turned cold and this time Katie invited him to come in. But Randy preferred to stay on the porch. Katie spread out an old blanket for him to lie on, and in the morning she rose early to feed him a bowl of warm porridge which she had prepared the night before.

These visits went on into the middle of November. They became more and more frequent. Each time Randy went away, Katie eagerly looked forward to his return. She also bought a large bag of dog food so that he could have a good meal when he arrived.

They began taking short walks together. The old woman moved slowly, and when Randy got too far ahead, he waited for her to catch up.

Before long he came into the house and slept beside her bed every night, stretched out on a large flowered pad she had made for him. She also bought herself a warm mackinaw and new, comfortable shoes.

Soon they were walking together every day. The old woman stepped more briskly now to keep up with her dog. Randy shortened his stride to help her.

When spring came, with the aid of a neighbor, Katie put in a vegetable garden and planted flowers along the front of the house. Later that summer she had the house painted white with green trim.

Randy never roamed again. Everyone had thought he was just a lovable tramp who followed an endless trail to nowhere. But the truth of the matter appears to be that Randy had indeed been in search of something—someone who really needed him. When he found Katie Conklin, he was content to spend the rest of his life with her.

Facing page: *An eight-week-old pup raises its head to take a whiff of the fresh spring air in a field of dandelions in the western United States. Photograph © Henry H. Holdsworth/Wild by Nature* Overleaf: *A button-nosed pup reclines amongst autumn leaves. Photograph © Alan and Sandy Carey*

Sailing with Sam

by Ann Raincock

A golden retriever changes the dynamics of life in an instant: Insert a friendly furball of a golden into a family and the experiences, the connections with others, and all of the otherwise mundane details of human existence become that much more textured, that much more thrilling.

Ann Raincock shared fourteen years of her life with a golden retriever named Sam, learning from the very beginning how much her loving, quiet golden added to her family's experiences. Raincock is the editor of *TravelScoop*, a Toronto-based newsletter aimed at independent travelers. Her work has also appeared in the publications *Canadian Yachting*, the *Globe & Mail* (Toronto), *Chatelaine Travels!*, *Doctor's Review*, and *DogGone*.

"Sailing with Sam" originally appeared in *Travelers' Tales: A Dog's World* (1998), edited by Christine Hunsicker.

Already sopping wet, a patient golden waits for another trip on, or into, the water. Photograph © Sharon Eide/Elizabeth Flynn

IT WAS THE children, of course, who saw it—a card pinned up on a notice board in the little general store close to the harbor. We were killing time, waiting for the aftermath of Hurricane Claus to pass us by. Outside the fishing boats of Menemsha strained and creaked on their lines, gray waves crashed over the harbor wall, and the rain fell in slanting gusts. No boats would leave that day and an afternoon confined to our own, while the rain beat on the decks above and condensation dripped below, was not an appealing prospect. I tried to gain some culinary inspiration from the meager display of tinned foods while my husband flicked through the store's magazines and the children read the cards on the wall.

"There's a notice over there." The younger one had appeared at my side looking sheepish.

"What does it say?" I asked him.

"Golden retriever pups for sale."

Silence. He traced a design on the dusty floor with his damp shoe. Then he took a deep breath.

"Can we buy one?"

I could hear his sister fidgeting from foot to foot in the aisle behind us, listening.

"No, my love," I laughed gently, putting my arm around his shoulders and drawing him towards me. "That really wouldn't be a good idea—not under the circumstances."

"The children saw an advertisement for golden retriever pups back in the store," I said quietly to my husband later. The children were in the aft cabin reading. "What do you think?"

"What do I think?" he echoed in amazement. "Are you crazy? Here are four of us confined to a sail boat, over a year of traveling still ahead of us, and you want a dog—a puppy? He'd need training, and walks, and visits to the vet, and bags of food, and bowls, and . . . and. . . ." he sputtered to a halt, catching his breath before continuing. "You must be out of your mind . . . all of you . . . no . . . absolutely, definitely no!" His raised voice had brought the children from their cabin.

Four hours later we wrote a check and received in return a small, warm, furry bundle with bright eyes and a black, wet nose. He had been born in Washington D.C. nearly seven weeks earlier and his owners had brought him, along with his brother, sister, and mother, to their summer home on Martha's Vineyard, hoping to sell the puppies there. After our telephone call they had immediately driven the dogs to the general store near the harbor to meet us. We had huddled out of the rain under the porch talking while the children had sat, speechless with excitement, on the old seat outside the store with the three puppies wriggling on their laps.

"Which one is it to be?" their father had asked.

Our daughter had shrugged her shoulders, eyes wide. This was no time to get into an argument with her more opinionated brother; everything at this meeting must run smoothly.

"This one," said her brother firmly, indicating the darker male. "Definitely this one."

And so he came with us. He was destined to grow up on a sail boat and to travel over 6,000 miles in the first year of his life. And he was destined, too, to change our lives and to bring a new dimension to our long-planned sailing adventure. But first, on that blustery afternoon, we took him on board and showed him his new home. Then we put a cushion in a corner of the main cabin where he promptly fell asleep, while the children settled down to watch him for hours until he awoke. While he slept we talked quietly and decided to call him Sam; Sailor Sam.

By the next morning the wind had diminished and the Sound was calmer; it was time to leave. We maneuvered out of our dock and set sail for Newport, Rhode Island, with Sam snuggled against the breeze on one lap or another. The pattern of that day was to repeat itself often in the days to come as we criss-crossed the Sound on our journey back to New York, before heading south for a year. For Sam, each day presented a new challenge: climbing on board from a variety of docks, scrambling out of the cockpit onto the deck, disentangling himself from a bundle of lines inadvertently dropped on him, and negotiating the steep steps of the companionway to the safety of "down below." When at anchor we used an inflatable dinghy to go ashore. Of course while small he could be lifted and passed down and up again, but the day would come when he'd have to jump. And jump he did, as soon as he was able.

The decision of when to let him take his first swim was made for us when, eager to reach the beach, he mistimed his disembarkation from

The golden is a powerful swimmer; this golden would likely be banned from no-wake zones Photograph © Henry H. Holdsworth/Wild by Nature

the dinghy and flung himself into the water. He was to swim almost every day of the trip from then on, becoming strong and powerful and able to keep his head underwater for considerable periods of time while attempting to retrieve a stone or some other interesting item from the bottom.

That first summer of our trip was drawing to a close as we motored down the East River, past Manhattan's Battery Point and turned to the south. By now Sam was well trained and well accustomed to the cruising life. Except on rare occasions we stopped every night, anchoring in a quiet bay or taking a berth at a marina.

Then, in fair weather or foul, we would ride ashore in the dinghy or disembark on the dock to take him for a walk, discovering many delights which we might otherwise have missed had we stayed on board. When we were late, and conscious that he might be uncomfortable, we would try to encourage him to relieve himself on deck (where a quick bucket of water would have taken care of the clean-up) but he never would and we respected him for that.

As the fall months passed we made our way down the eastern seaboard. We found a vet in Maryland for the necessary shots and a check up and everywhere we went we made new friends. He was a great conversation starter; all the people we met, whether ashore or on other boats, wanted to know how we had acquired Sam. And he was good, oh so very good. When we rented a car and took the children to Washington he thought this novel mode of transportation a great treat. And when we left him to sleep soundly on the back seat while we visited some museums there he patiently complied. He was a quiet dog, not stirring in the morning until someone in the family did, and rarely barking unless to encourage the dolphins that would soon come and play in our wake as we traveled through the Carolinas and beyond. Although very active, he also loved to sit beside the children, head on lap or sandy feet while the obligatory school work was done and in this way he helped to curb the children's restlessness.

We crossed the Gulf Stream from Fort Lauderdale to the Bahamas two days before Christmas and would not leave that island nation for five months. There Sam came to believe that life was, indeed, a beach. There he would swim and dive and run, or engage in his ongoing project—always interrupted by his family impatient to move on—of digging a hole to Australia. But life was not always perfect. One day, as we splashed through the shallows at Green Turtle Key in the Abacos searching for shells, a dark object swimming nearby caught Sam's attention. The young stingray darted away with Sam in hot pursuit and all the shouting and whistling in the world would have been to no avail. As we ran we watched in horror as Sam reached his prey. For what seemed like a very long time, but was probably only seconds, we witnessed the golden dog and the writhing gray wings come together, jumping, twisting, and thrashing in showers of silver spray. Then the ray hit his target and was gone. Sam yelped and lay down in the shallow water, examining his foreleg in confusion. He had only wanted to play. When we reached him we discovered he had been hit; the ray's barbed "sting" was firmly embedded in his leg.

A golden portrait. From the original oil painting by Robert K. Abbett. Reprinted by permission of the artist.

There was no other course of action available to us; without benefit of professional medical help the sting would have to be pushed through the leg and removed from the other side. So that is what we did. He bore it stoically and soon we were carrying him across the sun-dappled shallows with heavy hearts. Had muscles or tendons been severed? Would he suffer permanent damage? How could we prevent the wound from becoming infected? We were relieved that he had not been hit more horribly—in the head or, worse, the eye—but we were worried nonetheless. Yet his recovery was swift. He licked the wound himself and it quickly healed, leaving no discernible damage to the leg. My daughter still has the barbed sting, kept carefully in a tiny box among her shell collection.

Together we shared many hours of pure perfection and a few hours of grave concern. Once, on encountering an unexpected storm on the Bahama bank, my husband indicated to me that he would like the children to be below. "I don't like Sam being up here in this very rough weather," I was able to say to them. "Why don't you both go and snuggle up in the V-berth and keep him safe and calm until we're through this bad weather?"

All too soon we had to plan our return; our adventure was coming to an end and, fourteen months after our departure, we were to return to our urban life in Toronto, Canada. Another new world was waiting for Sam: the cold and snow of a northern winter, sleeping in a house, walking in a busy street, and being confined to a garden where he was not allowed to try digging to Australia.

Today, nearly twelve years after that wet windy afternoon on Martha's Vineyard, Sam is still with us. The children are grown-up now and much has changed, but every summer we all move aboard the boat docked on Toronto Islands. There Sam passes lazy days watching the ducks and snoozing on deck in the sun, waiting for us to return from our various daily activities. We call "Yo, Sailor Sam," as we approach and then he stirs, stretches and comes, tail wagging, to the bow to greet us and we know he is happy; this really is his home. For early every spring, when the snow has nearly gone and the days are getting longer, Sam becomes uncharacteristically restless. Then we put him in the car and drive down to the still-icy lake and show him the old boat and tell him that summer is coming.

A golden pup rests on a pier. Photograph © William H. Mullins

Where Dogs Come From

by Joseph Monninger

Golden retrievers add a little something to the course of life. It's tough to put your finger on what that little something is, but it's there whenever a golden is in the room, whenever a golden is by your side. If you think about it awhile, the answer will come to you: it's happiness. By its very nature, a golden creates happiness. And no matter how difficult life becomes, a golden in the mix automatically elevates the mood to create the golden life.

Joseph Monninger knows the golden life. A teacher by training and a writer and fly fisherman by inclination, Monninger has shared a good portion of his adult life with a golden retriever named Nellie. Monninger is the author of eight novels, including *The Family Man* (1982), *New Jersey* (1986), *Incident at Potter's Bridge* (1991), and *Mather* (1995).

"Where Dogs Come From," which tells the story of the author's fly-fishing trip in the American West with his golden retriever Nellie, first appeared in Monninger's beautiful 1999 memoir, *Home Waters: Fishing with an Old Friend.*

Living the golden life. Photograph © Bill Buckley/The Green Agency

DOGS ARE A standing introduction. I knew that once, but had forgotten it somewhere along the line. A man traveling alone in a pickup truck wearing khaki shorts and a baseball cap is often the object of suspicion. But a man traveling with an attractive dog, and a clear intent to fish, is another matter altogether. The first night out, at Lake Erie State Park in western New York, I tied Nellie to a long lead attached to the picnic table in our small camping spot. I fed her, gave her water, then busied myself setting up sleeping arrangements. It's a distinct pleasure, and a bit disorienting, to find yourself putting into practice what you had planned for months beforehand. Although I had brought a tent along, my design was to sleep in my truck on an old cot that I had packed for that purpose. To make room, however, I had to unload nearly everything and pile it on top of the fiberglass truck cap or squeeze it into the front cab. Before five minutes had passed, I realized I had turned my truck into what used to be known in California as a surfing safari wagon. With an inflated float tube on top, plastic vats of dog food and cereal, waders, flippers, a box containing my flytying gear, I was clearly designated as a man going fishing. Even the campground host, who had taken my ten dollars and pointed me to the appropriate tent slot, swung by again on his golf cart and asked where I was going fishing, how long I would be out. When I told him my idea for the trip, he related some of his own fish stories, again providing me with a place that couldn't miss, a place where the trout did the back stroke and waited to oblige fishermen.

But it was Nellie who made the most friends. At the end of her lead, she stretched to sniff the hands of a pack of children who came by, their fingers coated with marshmallow goo. In the campfire dimness, the children circled her and spoiled her, then ran off to wash for bed. Their place was taken by an older woman who passed with a towel around her neck and a flowered shower kit in her hand. She was at least sixty, apparently alone; I had seen her sitting at her own picnic table beside a minivan with Wisconsin plates. Switching her shower kit into her left hand, she bent to pet Nellie, who continued to strain at the end of her lead. When the woman stood, she said to me, "Nice dog." Then she shifted her towel around her neck again.

That was all it took. Nellie had served to introduce us, and for the next half hour the woman, whose name was Ronnette, kept one hand on my dog's back, the other on her towel. She told me she was on her way to visit her granddaughter, brand new, who had been born three weeks before. She said she was going to Massachusetts, heading the other way, east to my west, and she had considered flying but it had been years since she had taken a long drive and, besides, she actually liked to camp a little. She had camped often with her husband, Ben, who had died three years ago. They had owned a collie once, a black and white one, not a brown and white one like Lassie, and it had been a wonderful dog, but prone to chewing, especially when left alone.

Nellie gave her complete attention to Ronnette, except when the children passed by and again fussed over her. When the children departed, Ronnette said that her collie, KoKo, had died a long time ago, probably somewhere in the middle eighties. Then she thought about it for a second and tried to remember exactly, performing that curious exercise that

Happy days jogging on the beach. Photograph © Lon E. Lauber

Fisherman and friend casting for the catch of the day. Photograph © Alan and Sandy Carey

dogs seem to draw out of people. Dogs, I knew, were about time. For most people a dog recalled a specific period, and I would find, throughout my trip, that people who encountered Nellie told me about their own dogs, then inevitably remembered the dog's death. And when the people spoke about their dog's ending, they almost always kept one hand on Nellie, their eyes looking off in the distance.

When Ronnette went back to her camp, I spent a little while tying flies. I am an atrocious flytier, but I like the idea of doing it even if I am ham-handed. Besides, I needed to replenish my fly box. I clamped my vise to the picnic table and began tying my specialty, a triple-hackled trico. It's my specialty because it is the simplest fly a person can tie. After wrapping glitter around the stem of the hook, I topped the shank with three hackles. The hackles go on in a straightforward manner—dark, white, dark. The triple hackle, in addition to being a simple fly to tie, represents nearly anything moving in the water. It is as close as one can come to a universal fly. I tied it in the darkness by the light of a headlamp. The poor lighting might have been an excuse for a better flytier, but my flies came out as poorly as they always did. Nellie wandered around at the end of her lead. The campground grew more quiet. I finished four flies before calling it a night. By then the campfires had begun to die and I smelled their sweet fragrance, the scent of an encampment. Now and then I saw the silhouettes of people standing in their tents, preparing for bed. The crickets hardly spoke.

I took Nellie for a final walk. She is good about such things. I can say "last walk" and she knows it is time to be serious. We walked through the campground, then wandered over to a wide patch of grass. The grass led to a meadow, which in turn led to a group of power line stanchions.

From there, I figured, you could walk for miles.

At a safe distance from the campground, I let her off her lead. She walked with the high-gaited step she sometimes uses when the grass is wet. She inspected the hedgerow, the dense dam of bushes that pushed out from the uncut patches of growth. She has always liked, as most dogs do, the green tidal zone where forest meets meadow. She spent a few minutes sniffing and wading through the olive-colored grass. She looked beautiful in the meadow, the moonlight picking her up enough to reveal her fine coat, the white puff of a tail. She found a certain bush that held her interest, then she gave it up and circled around until she concluded her nightly chores. We stood for a while afterward and looked around. Someone once told me that Charles Darwin speculated that eighty percent of the planet's population does not lift its eyes above the horizon once a day. Whether true or not, whether Darwin ever said it or not, the quote has stuck in my brain and I have made it my routine to look up at least once every twenty-four hours. More often than not, I use my last walk with Nellie each night to survey the stars. I have learned the stars' names, at least some of them, a hundred different times, but invariably I forget them a month later. I know the North Star. I know a few of the planets. But I have decided, in recent years, that it is okay to fail at the constellations, consoling myself that names don't change the nature of a thing. The stars don't alter no matter what we call them, so now, when people from the cities visit, I tell them all manner of nonsense, inventing names on the spot.

Nellie, I have noticed, rarely looks above the horizon. I am not sure she has ever done so in her life. I have tried, at various times, to get her interested in a stellar phenomenon—I wondered, for example, if she would have any reaction to Hale-Bopp—but she appears to be oblivious. Standing next to her in the field, I let my hand dangle on her head. I rubbed the space between her eyes, then tickled the top of her skull. She sat and let me keep going. I played the

A golden retriever named Freeway lifts his head for pets from his owner. Photograph © J. Hatten Photo Illustrations

childhood game of blinking my left eye to make the stars jump one way, then my right eye to make them jump the other way. By doing it quickly, I could force one star to leap over the point of a pine.

We went back to the truck. Nellie walked easily on her leash. I hooked her to the towing ball while I cleaned the picnic table. I packed up everything, stowing it as carefully as I could, and realized, as I did so, that much of traveling is fussing. I put what I could on the roof of the truck, keeping things off the ground and away from raccoons. I figured we would have a frost. It was likely I would have frost every night from now on.

When I finished wrapping up camp, I put down the tailgate and let Nellie leap in first. I had set up an L.L. Bean cedar dog bed next to the cot, but naturally she preferred my bed. She curled into a ball on top of my sleeping bag and tried to ignore me. She went limp on purpose, hogging everything, which is a terrible trick she likes to play. I climbed in and shoveled her off, but not without an awkward struggle. Eventually I yanked the tailgate up and we were in, buttoned up for the night. A nice breeze lifted off Lake Erie. This cot was home for the next month, I told Nellie, but she didn't appear to pay attention. I turned this way and that, settling in, adjusting to the sensation—familiar but always surprisingly constricting—of sleeping in a mummy bag.

I flicked on my headlamp and read a bit from *So Little Time* by John Marquand. I nearly always bring Marquand on camping trips, not only because I admire him so, but because his books are about martinis and weekends in other people's houses. His books are like portable black-and-white movies, the best kind, and nearly as important, they take time to read. You don't want a short, snappy book on a camping trip.

After a while I turned off the headlamp and put Marquand aside. For a time I stayed awake, nervous and eager, happy to be started but also aware that no one in the world knew where I was at that moment. I reached down and put my hand on Nellie's rising ribs. She rolled over to have her belly rubbed, but I was too tired to oblige her. I fell asleep to her paw gently cuffing my wrist, trying to get my hand started.

I was living with my wife, Amy, at the St. Paul's School in Concord, New Hampshire, when we decided to get a dog. It was August. Earlier that summer we had been house-sitting in Putney, Vermont, and our daily walk had taken us past a beautiful antique Cape with the requisite Golden Retriever outside. The retriever was old, and somewhat unsteady on her feet, but she invariably barked twice when we arrived, rose to a standing position, her back hips obviously arthritic, then tottered toward us, her tail going. It was a highlight of our walk, if not of our entire day. We didn't know the dog's name, but because she was so reticent to come forward, and because she barked at us every single day, one of us named her Shy Girl. The name stuck. From that point on, whenever we talked about the possibility of getting a dog, we talked about Shy Girl.

If dogs are about time, they are also about the romance of steadiness. In American mythology, dogs come with screen doors that slam, swing sets, leaf raking parties, and jack-o-lanterns. For many of us, we want the idea of a dog long before we want the dog itself. Shy Girl,

A golden waits for her owner in the bed of a pickup on a snowy, sloppy day. Photograph © Lon E. Lauber

Pigtails and puppies make the world go 'round. Photograph © Jerry Irwin

although she was a loving dog and entirely wonderful in her own right, was also a symbol for us. We had met approximately ten years earlier and since then we had lived in Africa, Vienna, and New York. Our travel had been exciting, but we had failed to set roots. In our summers as teachers, we had led student groups to Australia, New Zealand, Canada, Holland, England, and France. Suddenly, however, we were thirty-five years old with a limited bank account, no permanent home, and a growing suspicion that we needed to settle into something lasting.

St. Paul's seemed to answer that need. Amy took a position as an English teacher, and as a dorm mom, while I taught as a visiting professor at the University of New Hampshire. We were given wonderful accommodations in Friendly House, the old converted servants' quarters, and were put in charge of forty or fifty girls. Amy was gifted as a student advisor. On dorm duty every second or third night, she made a fire in our living room, sat at an old oak table with her work spread in front of her, and counseled students, joked with them, talked about boys, took temperatures, and, in her quiet moments, wrote lavishly on their themes and papers.

I think, perhaps, we got a dog instead of having a child. I also think we knew, on some level, what we were doing, though neither one of us admitted it at the time. I'm certain the people around us, on hearing that we were getting a dog, probably rolled their eyes and said we should be having children instead. Looking back, I've often thought that we remained childless because we each silently suspected that we were not staying together. We told each other, surrounded by children, that we needed none of our own.

A dog was another matter. The arguments for a dog were compelling. St. Paul's has always been overrun with dogs. The school is set on an exquisite campus, approximately 118 acres of New Hampshire meadows, forests, and lakes. Faculty and staff tend to stay for years, giving the entire school a sense of continuity. When a groomer friend mentioned that a friend of a friend had just come into a first-rate litter of Golden Retrievers, we didn't hesitate. It was time for a dog.

On a bright September Saturday morning, the first chill of autumn making us sit outside and find the sun while we drank our coffee, we left St. Paul's to get Nellie. We had both had beagles as kids, Amy's dog named Cookie, mine named Porky, but that had been years ago. On the phone, the trainer had said we could have Brown Boy, a male, for $400. She said we could take a female for $200, but that the breeders required an agreement that the bitch not be neutered, and that the breeder got to pick the first and third pup from a litter. The trainer also said the breeders had a specialist supervising the dogs' breed characteristics, and that they would find a suitable mate after the female passed through two estrous cycles. We listened to all this information about reproduction half-heartedly. Against all advice to the contrary—new dogs owners generally do better with females because females tend to be less dominant—we wanted a male.

We drove along Route 7 to a beautiful farmhouse in southern New Hampshire and stepped out of the car to find a litter of Golden Retriever puppies wobbling around a spacious lawn. What had been a prospecting

The eyes of a tired golden resting her head on the lawn. Photograph © William H. Mullins

trip—maybe we'd get a dog, maybe we wouldn't—rapidly became a shopping trip. We were sunk. The puppies were ten weeks old and ridiculously cute. Brown Boy, when the trainer pointed him out, was a large, frumpy piece of fur. He was very sweet, but somehow, whenever we looked around, a small female seemed to be trailing us. She had a thinner face than Brown Boy, but she also seemed more alert. On our knees on either side of the pack, we asked the trainer to explain again the conditions for a female. She did. Then she left us alone to think about which dog we might like.

The dogs wandered between us, wrestling and sleeping almost at random, and we watched them closely. I wish that Amy and I had talked more about what was going on, what the dogs represented, but I suppose it is the nature of divorce that it has its beginnings in many things, not all of them knowable. Dogs are about time, as I've said, and at that time we wanted a dog. Neither of us was wise enough to look behind that desire.

Nellie was the one we wanted. Her official American Kennel Club name was Star Lake Nell. She came from a litter in Hanover, up near Dartmouth. We wrote a check, agreed to all the conditions concerning reproduction, then bundled her into the car. Amy drove and I kept Nellie entertained on my lap until she fell asleep. Her fur was soft and she smelled like doughnuts.

I read books on dog obedience and worked hard on making her sit, come, stay, heel. We crate-trained her. In the afternoons or the early evenings, we walked her all over the school grounds, going through the Pillsbury fields, the long trail along Turkey Pond, and even the trout stream in the center of campus. A young teaching intern named John had just acquired a black Lab puppy named Gusty, so we walked frequently with them, letting the dogs run and wrestle, their bodies nearly inexhaustible. If dogs did nothing else for us except force us to take to the fields and rivers in all kinds of weather, that would surely be enough.

It's likely I spent too much time with Nellie, that I relied too much on her companionship, because my wife and I had started to drift apart. In our continued effort to put down roots, an effort that would prove futile, we bought a century-old home on Port Hood Island, Nova Scotia. It had belonged to a lobsterman originally and had remained in his family for three generations. Financially, it was a crazy move and caused incredible strain in our marriage. We lived fourteen hours of hard driving away from the house. We would have been far wiser to have purchased a house in northern New Hampshire where we might have had good weekends away from the confinement of prep school life, but our vision was that we would spend the summers at the island house, improving it gradually every year. Besides, the house overlooked the sea, with wide grass fields sloping down to an incredible blue. It was a place, we thought, to make a stand. We would teach in New Hampshire through the fall and spring, then spend glorious summers on an island of grass and ocean. The same house on the Maine coast, we liked to tell each other, would be worth several million dollars.

Nellie was part of that house. She came with us when we drove up that first summer. She was able to swim whenever she liked, dipping down to the ocean that ran up onto our land. During the hotter parts of the day, she sat in the shade, looking out at the birds and boats. I converted a fishing shed to a writing room, the old gray beams hung with lobster gear, and Nellie spent her mornings with me there, laying in the sunny doorway, tail ready to greet anyone who came by. In the evenings we played croquet with the kids on the island, Nellie constantly sneaking in to run off with one of the colorful balls. A picture of those evenings, with the island kids barefoot, the adults watching the game on Adirondack chairs, Nellie running freely, the sea everywhere, can still fill me with longing.

One morning in the middle of our first summer on the island, when Bert Smith, our local caretaker, and I were approximately a half mile out to sea checking his mackerel nets, I turned to look landward and saw a wake coming toward me. Occasionally we saw what the locals called "black fish," or harbor whales, and I told Bert we had one approaching. But when I looked again and squinted against the morning glare, I realized it was Nellie. She was nine months old. She had seen me go to sea, so she had gone to sea. She was swimming after me, her ears spread on the surface of the sea, her breathing a *chaaa chaaa chaaa,* her paws paddling endlessly through the swells. She had been swimming for the better part of an hour at least, her gaze fixed on me. We pulled her into the boat and I fussed over her while she shook off the water. Nellie, like most dogs, simply accepted that I had forgotten her, that she had rectified the situation, and now we could go on with the day. Watching her shake off in the sun, Bertie said he had seen deer sometimes swimming miles off shore, driven to the sea by insects, then swept out by currents. He said he had seen a deer go down that way, its antlers sinking below

Jeff

by Howard Ogden

Jeff was a big golden retriever who lived to hunt pheasant. He would begin to shiver with anticipation the minute his master opened the closet door and reached for the shotgun. He would get even more frantic as preparations continued, and by the time the gear had been loaded into the car, he would be beside himself. Along the route to the game preserve his excitement would reach a fever pitch, and the car would have to be pulled over so he could get out and vomit—always at the same spot along the route (dogs being creatures of habit). Thus relieved, Jeff would become visibly calmer and more businesslike.

Jeff was an excellent bird dog and he performed his job with skill and enthusiasm. But when the hunt was over, he would become positively morose, almost belligerent. And he did not suffer novice hunters gladly: on one occasion I'm afraid I ruined Jeff's day. After having missed all my shots, I was handed his leash and was asked to lead him to the car, but Jeff stubbornly refused to budge. When I tugged harder he emitted a basso profundo growl that clearly said, "Pull me again, bozo, and I'll rip your throat out."

Eventually the gear was put back in the car and it was time to head for home. At his master's command, Jeff would get into the car slowly, as if he had aged considerably since that morning, when he had bounded into the back seat. He looked dejected, as if dreading the return to the safe, monotonous life of a family dog. Scrunched down in the back with his chin on his paws, he would fall into sullen sleep as the car turned onto the highway.

Howard Ogden is a California-based freelance writer.

Autumn days afield. From the original oil painting by Eldridge Hardie. Reprinted by permission of the artist.

With a gangly arm like that of your average human teenager, a pup sprawls on a lichen-bedecked stone. Photograph © Alan and Sandy Carey

the surface until a last survival impulse pushed it up again, its antlers butting against heaven before it dropped finally into the sea water.

When I told Nellie's story later to a friend, she remarked that love, if it was anything, was the ability not to hesitate. She said Nellie had fetched her heart to me and that she would always find me wherever I went. She said the fact that Nellie did not think when she came to the water, did not weigh anything, but simply followed what she loved, was something, ultimately, to be envied.

We lost the island house in the divorce. On teachers' salaries, neither one of us was able to maintain a summer residence so far removed from our daily lives. We sold the house and divided our other property, including our pets. Amy took an old tomcat named Gray Man. I took Nellie. I had spent more time with her, had trained her, and, in some way, needed a dog in a way Amy did not. After thirteen years together, I moved out with the contents of one pickup truck, Nellie on the seat beside me.

Nellie and I arrived in Lander, Wyoming, at noon on our fourth day out. The entrance to Lander from the south is dramatic. The land turns red and begins to tuck closer to the road, forming a ruddy chute that drops from the plateau into a valley that contains the Wind River. At the brink of town, you begin to see fishing access signs. These signs are scattered all over the West. Brown and rectangular, with a white hook dangling in front of wide-eyed fish, they are somewhat torturous to pass, because each one seems promising. Fishermen use them to guide each other to good spots. Find the fishing access spot, then wade upstream, they will tell each other. I slowed as I passed each access point, not because I intended to fish them, but because I wanted to make mental notes. My short-term memory is abysmal and seems to get worse every year, but I have never had difficulties remembering fishing spots.

Nellie, when she felt the truck wind down at these signs, looked rapidly from me to the road. She had been a good sport about the traveling, taking our short breaks well and chasing the Frisbee if I threw it, but she was bored. Most mornings she slept with her chin on my knee, but in the afternoons she was restless. Now, with the truck slowing to examine the fishing signs, she stood, then sat, then stood again. Her nose rubbed the windshield from inside. It was already streaked with a thousand nose marks, but she found a few new spots to mark. It did no good, at this point, to tell her to relax. She wanted out and I didn't blame her. Suddenly, we had arrived. We had seen the sky opening for the last two days and now it was bright above us, wide in a way that it is never wide in the East.

I pulled over not next to the river, but on a small dirt road heading into what appeared to be a ranch pushed up against the Wind River Range. Side roads are always best for running a dog and this one promised to be excellent. A cattle grate covered the intersection of the dirt road and the interstate. On either side of the road, pale green sage spread for miles. As soon as I stopped the truck, I popped open the passenger door. Nellie flew off the seat, her body so eager to be moving she couldn't wait. By the time I climbed out, she was already down off the crest of the dirt road, her tail up, her nose skimming the ground. She galloped over the field, whisking through sage, her back legs impatient with her front legs,

Water break for a mountain biker and his golden sidekick in the mountains of Montana. Photograph © Bill Buckley/The Green Agency

so desperate was she to run. Now and then she stopped and looked at me, apparently not trusting her luck that she was free to run as long as she liked. I told her to go. She didn't need to be told twice.

I opened the tailgate, pulled out sandwich fixings, and sat and watched. I had time to eat a peanut butter and jelly sandwich before she returned. She was winded. Her tongue lolled out of the right side of her mouth and her fur was dotted with burrs. I brushed her out, poured water for her, then gave her a couple of biscuits. She panted around, lapping the water and slopping things onto the dry ground before she finally found a spot in the shade under the tailgate. She flumped onto the dirt and reclined backward, happy to have a run, happy to be cool in the white soil. As always, it surprised me that she had no further expectation. If I had decided to stay the next two months in my truck, living on peanut butter and jelly and reading books on my tailgate, she would have remained gladly beside me. If I moved to Boston and decided to take a small apartment, she would have lived with me there.

We drove into town a little later. Lander, like many towns in the West, has undergone a conversion to the eco-trade, adventure travel business that sustains many western regions in a manner ranching would be hard pressed to match. The fleece economy, a friend of mine calls it, referring to the preferred clothing of the clients. NOLS, an organization for outdoor learning, is headquartered in Lander, and you can almost always spot the people who work there, most of them driving Jeeps and wearing expensive sunglasses. Lander's streets are wide and dotted with tourist shops selling postcards, disposable cameras, and Native American gear. There are also several taxidermy stores, some with signs saying they are willing to trade antlers. Signs throughout Wyoming tell you how far you are from Yellowstone, and Lander is no exception. Lander is not a destination anywhere near as popular as Yellowstone, but it is becoming more popular, which subjects it to the kind of Catch-22 that threatens hot places for the fleece trade. Drawn to out-of-the-way places, the fleece trade invades an area until it becomes overrun by other fleece traders. Gradually, then, it becomes less interesting, less remote in the best sense, and becomes less appealing to a group of people who define themselves by the status gained by getting away from it all. The same principle, unfortunately, can often be applied to anglers.

Nellie and I had the afternoon to kill while we waited for my longtime friend and fishing buddy, Bob Harvey, and his brother-in-law, Tom, whom I had never met. I parked in the center of town and found a spot on a bench in the sun. The heat felt good. Nellie curled up in a shady spot nearly underneath the bench and pretended to sleep. I looked at my watch. Bob and Tom were arriving from Salt Lake City near five. I had at least three hours on my hands. After a while I walked over to The Good Place, an outdoor shop specializing in fishing and hunting. I tied Nellie to a pole outside and went in to browse the topo maps. I hate appearing like a sport, an easterner who has come out West on holiday, but it was unavoidable. Eventually one of the store clerks came over to help me. She said Bears Ear, the trail we intended to take the next day, was a great hike. She also said the Popo Agie River ran at the end of town and if I had an afternoon to kill, it wouldn't be a bad place to get out the kinks.

I paid for a license, which I needed anyway, then followed her directions out to the edge of town. Nellie guessed what was up and had the jitters at the thought of taking a swim. We found a brown sign that indicated fishing access and parked in a square dirt lot. The sun was still hot.

It took me a while to dig my fishing equipment out of the truck bed. Nellie, impatient for the water, kept running to the cattle fence that lined the bank, inspecting it, then running back to me. The water, when I looked in that direction, appeared a metal shelf, a glinting rigid blade stabbed through brown hills and brush.

It took ten minutes to get rigged up. I gave Nellie a biscuit that she hardly tasted. She wanted the water and that was all. When I slapped my thigh to tell her I was ready, she darted off and slipped under a strand of barbed wire, performing a GI crawl I didn't know she knew how to do. I carried a five-weight rod down to the river. As I approached, the water softened. It was no longer metal, but liquid instead, the melt of sun on rock and brown grasses. Crickets frittered up and into the light. Behind me black mountains stretched in a line toward the horizon. The land smelled of cattle and barns and corn.

Nellie waited for me chest deep in the river. She often ruins good fishing holes, but her company is worth it to me. I told her, though, that she would have to swim upstream or downstream but she didn't listen. She bent and lapped at the water, refreshed after our long days of driving.

The Popo Agie, the section on the outskirts of Lander, was small and beautiful. It rolled back and forth, twisting over farm country, bordered, in most places, by barbed wire fences. I walked downstream a bit until I found what appeared to be a particularly deep hole. I unhooked my fly, a black gnat, and cast. The water met the fly and carried it, as each river does, toward the sea.

I did not fish particularly well. I was too conscious of my surroundings, of the fact that I was merely killing time, to concentrate properly on the river. I believe rivers and fish know such things—they detect a fake. Besides, I had never heard of the Popo Agie until an hour before, and I am skeptical of rivers until they prove themselves to me. I fished by form rather than with passion, hopeful but not avid. The real fishing hadn't begun, I told myself. Nellie wandered back and forth, exploring the sage and meadow grasses. It was good to have her out. She splashed quite a bit but I didn't blame her.

In two hours' fishing I did not have a nibble. The sun began to run on the water, taking an angle and tucking shadows next to rocks and into the ripples. Crickets whirled in the light and landed on the water, riding the current, passing from sun to shadow. I watched to see if a trout took them, but the crickets rode out of sight, bobbing downstream, impervious, eventually tricks of light and distance transforming them to water. I changed flies regularly, trying to match the insects, but never unlocked the river.

Around five I called Nellie and we went back to the truck. While I pulled off my waders, she had a good roll in the dust. We drove into town with the windows halfway up, cold slipping down from the mountains. I parked next to The Good Place, the rendezvous spot with Bob and Tom, and waited.

A golden retriever in front of a huge snowdrift on a crisp, clear winter day. Photograph © Lon E. Lauber

Rafting on the Middle Fork of Idaho's Salmon River. Photograph © William H. Mullins

The Wind River Range stretched all around us. I had been in the Winds before and knew some of their history. Though not as famous as the Grand Tetons, they are probably the greatest mountain range in Wyoming and arguably in the lower forty-eight states. The seven largest glaciers in the Rocky Mountain states are located in the Winds. Gannett Peak, at 13,804 feet, spikes the center of the range and is the highest peak in Wyoming. The Winds are granitic and separate the Green River basin to the south and west from the Wind River basin to the north and east. The range runs on a north-west diagonal along Route 287 from Atlantic City at the south end, up past Lander, Ft. Washakie, Crowheart, Burris, Dubois, eventually bleeding into the Grand Tetons at Moran Junction. On the southern rim, traveling Routes 189 and 191, you can hit Hoback Junction, Bondurant, and Pinedale. The range encompasses Shoshone National Forest, the Fitzpatrick Wilderness, Bridger National Forest, Bridger Wilderness, the Popo Agie Wilderness, and the Wind River Indian Reservation.

What we now call Wyoming is the land of Arapaho, Bannock, Blackfoot, Cheyenne, Crow, Sioux, Lakota, Ute, and Shoshone people. When French trappers began making their way down the rivers, sometime in the mid-1700s, the Indians were waiting for them, alerted by word of mouth. The Shoshone, who inhabited much of the Wind River area, were known as the "snake" Indians. They formed compact, isolated family groups, who collected seeds, roots, fish, birds, and small game such as rabbits in their proper season. They returned to the same areas once each year and referred to each other according to the main food source of a region. There were Seed Eaters, Rabbit Eaters, and so forth. If the family units had an abundance of food, they gathered together where winter was mild to form a village. After the Shoshone acquired horses from the Spaniards, they became buffalo hunters like the Plains tribes.

Sacagewea, who served as a guide and interpreter for Lewis and Clark, was a Shoshone. So were the chieftains Pocatello and Washakie. The Wind River Indian Reservation was presented to Chief Washakie in 1868 in return, our government said, for the Shoshone's friendliness to white people and their help in fighting tribes hostile to settlers. Washakie was buried in the town named after him, located halfway up the Winds. And it was near Ft. Washakie, just past the Wind River Indian Reservation, that Nellie and I were going to fish.

From inside the pickup we waited and watched the sun fade to a tired red, the long boulevard behind us growing shadowy and washed. Nellie nosed at a fly that had made its way to the dashboard. I reached into the truck bed and grabbed the green L.L. Bean dog pack I had already loaded with mittens and hats and her supply of dog food. I anchored it across her back by tightening the straps under her legs and across her chest. She sniffed at the pack, recognized it as hers, then looked straight ahead. *Hiking*, I told her, but she didn't seem to make much of that so I changed it to *Walk*. Immediately she perked up and stood, ready to go. I grabbed her front paws and made her dance the cha-cha a little. I put her ears above her head and told her she looked like a Russian peasant woman. She tolerated everything, although clearly she would have preferred a walk. The bear bells on her backpack tinkled whenever she moved.

First Fall

~

by Todd Tanner

The golden retriever was bred for hunting, for waterfowling, for fetching game. Today, the golden remains a first-class hunter both as a waterfowler, and, given the breed's patient temperament and excellent sense of smell, a very capable hunter of upland birds such as pheasant and grouse. Spending a little time pursuing game birds with a golden retriever by your side is yet another way to live the golden life.

Over the years, Todd Tanner has shared his life with five golden retrievers, including two today. An outdoors writer and occasional fishing and hunting guide based in Montana, Tanner has published his work in many of the leading sporting magazines, including *Field & Stream, Retriever Journal, Sporting Classics, Fly Fisherman, American Angler,* and *Fly Rod & Reel.* His writing has also appeared in several anthologies, including Voyageur Press's 1998 book *Love of Goldens: The Ultimate Tribute to Golden Retrievers.*

"First Fall" was originally published in the June/July 1998 issue of the *Retriever Journal.*

Todd Tanner's Cody. Cody "was a natural," Tanner writes, "and my single biggest achievement was not ruining his instincts." Photograph © Todd Tanner

WHEN I WAS 21, I decided I was done hunting birds. No more pheasants, no more grouse, no more woodcock. I believed, with the immutable certainty of youth, that my fowling days were over, that my passion for chasing whitetails with a stick and a string would carry me through to distant gray-haired retirement. In southern New York where I lived at the time, bird season and bow season pulled on the same time slot, and in keeping with my slightly obsessive personality, I gave up the cornfields and hedgerows for the prospect of a month long treetop vigil, secure in the knowledge that I was following the anointed path.

For 14 years I kept the faith, sneaking into my treestand one full, frigid hour before daylight and sitting there—unmoving—while I gradually lost sensation in my fingers and toes, all the while mouthing that silent bowhunter's mantra: "Just five more minutes . . . just five more minutes . . . just five more minutes." Eventually, though, my commitment wavered, and in the fall of 1995 (now living in Montana, where the bird and bow seasons are sensibly staggered), I fell prey to my friend Tim Linehan's constant urgings—"Give in to the dark side, young Skywalker"—and reached for my shotgun again.

It was all downhill from there.

My wife, Molly, and I picked up Cody from the breeder this past March, a tiny ball of golden fuzz with a mohawk between his eyes and a pedigree that screamed *Champion!* back six generations, and brought him home to Bozeman. While she never said it, I'm sure my wife took one look at Cody, the most promising pup of that litter of champion goldens, glanced at me—Mr. "I have no idea how to train a hunting dog"—and decided that we would soon be putting that tired old genetics vs. environment argument to rest.

Surprisingly, genetics won out.

By the end of October, when Steve "Mac" McFarland drove up from Utah with his black Lab, Boomer, Cody was showing more savvy and poise in the field than I had any right to expect. He'd already flushed a number of ruffed grouse (which I missed), three blue grouse (I missed those, too), and a half-dozen pheasants, several of which managed to show up on time for Sunday dinner. Cody listened, he worked close and hard, and he accomplished it all with a style and enthusiasm that went far beyond his nine months. While I'd love to take credit for his development, I didn't really have much to do with it; he was a natural, and my single biggest achievement was not ruining his instincts.

Central Montana, north and east of my Bozeman home, is a little like old pottery. From a distance it looks smooth and uniform, vast plains rising and falling with nature's irresistible rhythm, while the occasional mountain or butte suggests the craftsman's decorative touch. Up close, though, the cracks and chips become visible, and you can feel history stirring in the blemishes under your fingers.

Big Spring Creek flows through one of those cracks on the Montana plain, twisting through endless fields of wheat and giving life to both the farms and ranches that line its banks and the animals that drink

Muck flying, a golden leaps into a pond amidst a flock of decoys. Photograph © Bill Marchel

"Golden Puppy." From the original painting by Linda Picken. Reprinted by permission of the artist.

its cool, clean water. Mac and I drove north for the pheasants that roost in the cattail draws and willow thickets along the creek, hopeful that we'd find a few birds, watch the dogs work, and maybe get a shot or two.

Mac, who's a fly-fishing outfitter in the spring and summer, a big-game guide in the fall, and a ski instructor in the winter, doesn't get in much bird hunting because of his schedule. But he's one of those rare individuals so instinctively in tune with his environment that his lack of practice doesn't matter. He's slow, perceptive, and patient—about what you'd expect from a guy who makes his living chasing elk and trout—and an excellent shot to boot. More importantly, though, he doesn't care if the hunting's good, fair, or poor as long as he's out in the field enjoying himself. Boomer, though he runs a little heavy compared to Mac's lean frame, works birds the same way as his owner—easy, steady, and thorough.

We pulled up next to the grain silo, where the woman at the weather-beaten farmhouse had directed us to park (it's not always easy to get permission to hunt private land in Montana, but if you knock on enough doors, someone will usually give you the go ahead), and let the dogs out of my pickup. Cody started bounding around, your typical hyperactive juvenile golden, while Boomer stretched, pissed on my tire, and then sat down while we hauled our guns out. If Boomer, the mellowest six-year-old Lab I've ever met, could talk, he'd sport a Jamaican accent and tell you, "The pheasant, he's a peace-lovin' bird, mon. He don't like noise and jumpin' around. You got to sneak up on him nice and quiet-like if you want a shot."

And, more often than not, he'd be right.

There was prime cover just west of the silo, a half-mile-long field of CRP bordered by railroad tracks on the right and a row of cottonwoods on the left. Wheat fields stretched into the distance behind the trees, and a ditch filled with cattails paralleled the edge of the CRP.

We hadn't gone more than 50 yards from the truck when Cody started getting birdy, but he gave up too early and Boomer—Mr. Slow and Steady—put the hen up at our feet. The pup's a fast-learner though, and he flushed two more birds in the next few minutes—hens that held tight in the thick, thigh-high grass.

That was it until we reached a large clump of cattails near the end of the CRP. Cody started working harder, his tail switching from the side-to-side "life is good and I'm having fun" motion to that "a tornado ate my butt" explosion that sticks his nose into the ground and moves his body into overdrive. Even Boomer got excited, which meant that: one, we were about to hit the proverbial mother lode of Montana pheasants or; two, we were closing in on a covey of giant chicken-fried steaks. Luckily (my cholesterol is too high already), it turned out to be the former.

Boomer bumped the first bird from the cattails, a rooster that Mac toppled with one shot. We both swung on the second, and a lucky blast from my dad's old Belgian-made Browning dropped him. Then Cody, my puppy, my instinctive genius of a golden retriever, crashed off into the cattails, completely ignoring my pleading, "Cody, come! Find the bird," and within 30 seconds put up a dozen more roosters. All of which flushed just out of range. Later, back at the truck, Mac grinned and muttered something about fly-fishermen who train their dogs for catch and release. What could I say? Cody had the right idea. He just needed a little work on timing and restraint.

We spent the next couple of days in the same general area. Mornings and evenings we hunted CRP near the wheat fields, and in the heat of the day we dropped into the creek bottoms for birds roosting in the cattails and willows. Cody and Boomer started hunting as a team, the Lab doing heavy, power-forward work on the inside, the golden ranging back and forth like a point guard. It was something to see, especially when they converged on the same bird, and Mac and I had more shooting than we could have hoped for. For the first time since I was a teenager back in the seventies, I felt as if I had a real handle on pheasant hunting.

But the high point of the trip would come late one evening as we worked a hundred-acre patch of CRP near a harvested wheat field. Mac and I both had the satisfying weight of pheasants in our game vests, and the sun had just dropped below the western horizon. It was our last run of the day. Cody came racing in from my left flank, going full speed with his head held high. Then, almost as if someone had grabbed him by the nose, he pirouetted around and stopped dead three feet from a thick clump of grass. I yelled for Mac to get ready, and we both walked up as Cody stood frozen, his nostrils flared and sides quivering.

We weren't more than 20 feet away when Cody lunged and the pheasant flushed, heading straight into the sunset. I called out, "Hen!" and lowered my gun, but Mac fired and the bird pinwheeled to the ground and took off running. Cody gave chase, and both pheasant and dog disappeared in a tangle of cattails and willows on the edge of the field.

I turned to Mac and asked, "Are you sure that was a cockbird?"

"Positive—" he said. But before he could utter another word, Cody burst out of the thicket with the pheasant in his mouth. He came racing up and sat down in front of me, then released the bird on command. I handed Mac his rooster, a plump young cock brilliant with the colors of autumn, and then knelt down to scratch Cody's ears. "That's my boy," I told him. "That's my good boy." He smiled that infectious golden retriever grin, the one that always melts my heart, and I hugged him close. For a few moments there, life was damn near perfect.

Above: *A golden searches for pheasant in a robust barley field. Photograph © Henry H. Holdsworth/Wild by Nature*
Overleaf: *"The Snipe Hunter." From the original painting by Peter Corbin. Reprinted by permission of the artist.*

Canyon

by Gary Shiebler

Though many would argue—adamantly—that the golden retriever is the perfect dog, the golden is not completely "flawless"; some individual goldens can even be considered downright loopy. It just goes to show you that golden retrievers are no different than cats or Russian politicians: Collectively, they don't always do what you would like them to do, and individually, some are quite insane. This, too, is a part of the golden life.

Gary Shiebler grew up with goldens; his parents insisted at least two goldens be a part of the family throughout his childhood. Ever since, things have seemed a little off kilter for Shiebler without a golden around. He is the author of two books, including *A Search for the Perfect Dog* (1997), in which "Canyon" first appeared, and he is presently at work on a follow-up to that wonderful book. A singer and songwriter as well as an author, Shiebler has written songs for Patti LaBelle and other artists. He has also recorded his own music, including the CD *Papa Was a Fishing Man,* a collection of tunes devoted to the angling arts.

Shiebler's search for the perfect dog leads him to Canyon, a golden a little different than the one he had in mind when he began his quest.

The tall grasses of Wyoming's Teton Valley and a handsome golden. Photograph © Henry H. Holdsworth/ Wild by Nature

WHEN I WAS a boy, every morning before school my father made lunch for my brother and me. I can still see him standing in the kitchen in his pajamas, listening for baseball scores on the dusty radio that sat atop our refrigerator while he carefully assembled our sandwiches. Some days it was Virginia ham and Swiss cheese with mustard, other days roast beef with mayonnaise on a soft white roll. If we were really lucky, we'd unwrap our aluminum foil at school to discover last night's sirloin steak leftovers between two slices of Wonder bread with plenty of salt, pepper, and mayonnaise and a dash of Lea & Perrins. Each lunchtime held a tender mystery, and we were rarely disappointed.

Sometimes, hidden among the tiny red boxes of Sun-Maid raisins and plastic bags filled with vanilla wafers we'd find little notes or baseball scores. My dad knew that Roberto Clemente was my favorite player, so he always made sure I knew how many hits he had the night before.

"Three for Three" his little yellow note might say.

I have noticed that supermarkets offer an assortment of prefabricated lunches for children, packaged in bright and cheery boxes. They are perfectly neat, compact, and tidy. Convenient and easy. They contain anything from mini sandwiches, small squares of cheese, and tiny stacks of lunch meat to bite-size pieces of candy, brownies, and even miniature do-it-yourself cracker pizzas.

A few years back when I went in search of the perfect dog, I wanted one on the order of those prefab lunches—bright and cheery, neat, compact and tidy, convenient and easy. I didn't find one. In fact, I ended up with the exact opposite of what I was looking for—a big, goofy, fearful mess of a golden retriever named Canyon.

He is the dopiest, most uncoordinated wreck of an animal I have ever known.

After having lived with a very fearful and insecure dog for eleven years, I vowed that the next dog I got would be independent, sure, and strong. I thought I couldn't go wrong with a golden retriever.

"Overbreeding," my wife says.

Whatever the diagnosis, I am stuck with him. And he is stuck with me. (If it turns out to be scientifically valid that dogs are the true reflections of their owners, I will immediately go into counseling. With three dogs, I probably should anyway.)

I got Canyon about a month after Squeeze died. I felt guilty looking so soon. I probably rushed into it too quickly.

I just got tired of missing her.

Canyon was the first dog that I looked at. The ad said: "Beautiful young male golden retriever. AKC, $40.00." My daughter and I went to see him.

He had been dumped in a side yard and ignored for the better part of his one and a half years. When his owner walked him to the front yard, it was as if Canyon was seeing the outside world for the first time.

A voice inside me said, "No! He's too much work! He's too much work!"

A golden with a muzzleful of snow in the sunshine after a mid-winter storm. Photograph © Alan and Sandy Carey

At Least He Didn't Get the Book Thrown at Him

by Bruce Nash and Allan Zullo

A golden retriever named Wofford loves to sink his teeth into a good book—literally.

Unfortunately, his penchant for literary works landed him in court.

Wofford, owned by David Viccellio, of Norfolk, Virginia, has a thing about books. "Our family likes to read, so there are books everywhere," explained Viccellio. "Whenever a guest comes over, Wofford will pick up a book with his teeth and hand it to him. He just loves books, especially paperbacks." Other times, the book hound will curl up in a corner with a good book.

One day in 1993, the dog slipped through a broken slat in the backyard fence and sauntered over to the Larchmont branch library next door. The back door had been left open to catch a breeze, so Wofford trotted inside. Seeing all those books, Wofford couldn't resist taking one.

He snatched a children's book off a little table and, being a friendly pooch, headed over to where the people were—at the checkout counter.

"There he was, standing by the desk, "recalled Albert Ward of the library staff. "Waiting very patiently. Behaving like you should in a library."

After doing a double-take, one of the librarians called the phone number on Wofford's collar, hoping to talk to the owner. But no one was home. "I got a message on my answer machine that said, 'This is the library. Your dog is trying to check out a book and he doesn't have a card,'" recalled Viccellio. "In fact, the librarian left several messages and finally they called the animal control people."

Viccellio arrived moments before Wofford was going to be hauled off to the pound. The owner was handed the dog—and a summons to appear in court for having a dog at large and not having a dog license.

"I showed Wofford the summonses, and they got his attention," said Viccellio. "He was burying bones out in the yard. I guess he felt we weren't going to feed him if things went badly in court."

When Viccellio appeared before Judge William Oast, the judge read the details of the case and asked him, "Was the dog trying to take a book out of the library?"

"No, your honor," said Viccellio. "He wasn't taking it. He was in the checkout line when they found him."

"Well, that's good to hear," said Oast.

The understanding judge didn't throw the book at the dog. Instead, he dropped the charges against Wofford, but ordered Viccellio to pay court costs of $28.

Reading about the zany case in the newspapers, students at an elementary school in Virginia Beach, Virginia, gave Wofford a gift—his very own school library card.

Bruce Nash and Allan Zullo are freelance writers and the authors of Amazing But True Dog Tales *(1994), in which this story first appeared.*

Do you have any picture books about bones? Photograph © David Lorenz Winston

The author Gary Shiebler knows well the voracious and indiscriminate appetite of the golden retriever. This golden almost looks guilty gulping down his chow. Photograph © William H. Mullins

But I stayed and ventured in a little deeper.

These kinds of searches are affairs of the heart, and there seems to be a point of no turning back. Once I cross the boundary between caring and not caring, it's impossible for me to retreat to indifference. The moment I saw this terrified young dog, I felt a deep sense of responsibility and duty. It was clear that if I didn't take him, he would be returned to a place of loneliness, fear, and neglect. I couldn't walk away.

I decided to take him for a walk. He startled at almost everything—the rustle of a leaf in a tree, the slam of a car door. He almost leaped into my arms at the sight of a black garbage bag sitting in a driveway. He was like a newborn colt walking on a trail of rattlesnakes. I wondered whether he had ever left that side yard at all. I sat down on the curb and slowly pulled him over. My gentle pats and soft scratches echoed my daughter's promise.

"Don't worry, Canyon," she whispered. "We will take care of you."

We took him home. My wife was visibly disappointed. I couldn't blame her. He was a big project.

"We don't need any more big projects," she lamented.

For weeks, I tried to convince her.

"You know honey, he really is surprising me with his intelligence." I kept trying.

"You know sweetheart, you may laugh, but beneath that dopey demeanor is a very smart dog. . . . And don't forget, he's registered AKC."

"American Knucklehead Club," she said.

I couldn't argue. He was a complete and total knucklehead.

Rarely have I seen a golden that could not gracefully retrieve a stick or catch a ball. I have ceased to play fetch with him for fear he may seriously injure himself. I have thrown balls five feet in the air and watched him land flat on his back. I have seen him confidently run twenty-five feet past a freshly thrown stick. A while back, he tried to turn around on a small walking bridge at a county park and fell off into the dry riverbed a few feet below.

We will not be hiking in the Grand Canyon anytime soon.

His tail is a lethal weapon when it comes to potted plants, Christmas ornaments, and cups of tea. Even small children are fair game.

He is reduced to convulsive fits and tremors at the sound of a leash. Trying to put a collar around his neck for a walk resembles a vaudeville routine. He'll sit for a second, jump up, sit down again because he knows it's wrong to jump up, then try to jump into his collar like a circus dog through a flaming hoop, miss completely, sit down again, shake, whine, tremble, belch, look at me, look at the door, look at me, look at the door, look at me.

Even the other dogs watch in disbelief.

Once I get his collar on, getting from the kitchen to the front door can be an adventure in and of itself. The combination of paws and toenails on a linoleum floor is very similar to the skating clowns segment at the Ice Capades. There is no talking sense or calm into him. I have tried to make him sit at the door, hoping he might be able to gather himself before we go out.

It's too painful to watch.

He looks like a chicken who can't stop laying eggs.

I have known a number of golden retrievers in my life and am fully aware of their hearty appetites and nondiscriminating palates. I have seen them devour turkey breasts and pumpkin pies set too close to the edges of countertops, swipe sticks of butter from dinner tables, and inhale kibble from cat dishes in a matter of seconds. My father's golden, Honey, was like a goat. She would eat anything. One of my most vivid memories as a teenager is of watching my father pull a pair of my mother's panty hose from Honey's backside one Saturday morning. Fortunately,

Sandy tennis ball in mouth, a goofy golden catches a few rays at the beach. Photograph © Sharon Eide/Elizabeth Flynn

A "perfect" golden retriever profile. Photograph © William H. Mullins

Canyon has shown no interest in my wife's lingerie. He does, however, have a penchant for sweat socks, teddy bears, and small area rugs.

Like Squeeze, Brodie, and so many other dogs I have known, Canyon is most happy when chasing seagulls at the beach or galloping along trails in the forest. At these times, his true nature emerges. He sheds his clumsy ways, and many of his fears seem to evaporate into the skies. He becomes wise to the world around him—the air, the light, the earth. He is free. Free to do the things that dogs love to do.

It is a joy to behold.

When I first got Canyon, I was angry and disappointed with his behavior. I wanted him to be the perfect dog. But no matter what I said or did, he wouldn't change.

I tried to fix him. I read books. I sought counsel from friends. I listened to tapes in my car and rented videos. I took him to obedience class. Nothing worked.

Three months after I got him, I considered putting Canyon up for adoption. I was convinced that every dog on the other side of every fence was more obedient, better behaved, and less fearful than my own.

Then I started teaching at the animal center, where I met hundreds of dogs just like Canyon. Dogs who jumped up too much. Dogs who had too much energy. Dogs who barked too much. Dogs who were too much work. Dogs like Frazier and Champ and Cody. Orphans in a world filled with too many expectations and too little time. How close Canyon had come to being one of them.

Of all the lessons I learned during my time at the animal center, perhaps the greatest one is that imperfect dogs are no less worthy of love than are the so-called perfect ones. I had put this lesson into practice at the center but not in my relationship with my own dog. I suddenly realized it was time to stop searching for the perfect dog and start loving the one I had.

Tomorrow morning I will get up at about 6:30, walk bleary-eyed to the kitchen, and flick on the radio that sits atop the refrigerator. I will greet all the furry creatures gathered eagerly at my feet and maybe start some hot water for tea. I will yell for the first of many times to my daughter to get up as I begin to make her lunch. Peanut butter with a little marshmallow Fluff. I'll fill a Baggie with popcorn, cut up a kiwi, and wrap a piece of homemade corn bread in some foil.

"C'mon Hayden. . . . Time to get up!"

And when she opens her lunch at school that day, not just food will spill out on the table. A whole bunch of love will as well. If she's lucky, she might even find a Garfield cartoon.

As for Canyon, he will never be the dog who waits patiently in the back of my pickup while I sip coffee with a couple buddies at the local diner. He will never be a finalist in any Frisbee-catching contest. He will most likely not be the dog that sits obediently at my feet while I relax in my favorite chair reading the evening paper. He may never be the fearless, majestic, heroic dog of my dreams—the perfect dog.

But then, I will never be the perfect owner.

What a relief.

Part III:

A Nose for Trouble and a Helping Hand

"The most golden part of a golden retriever is his heart."
Roger Caras, in the foreword to *Love of Goldens,* 1998

Left: *Determination, a top-notch sense of smell, and an overwhelming need to please make the golden retriever a leader in many activities that aid humankind. Photograph © Lon E. Lauber*
Above: *Adrift in a sea of dandelions, a golden breathes in the fragrant air. Photograph © Henry H. Holdsworth/Wild by Nature*

Nosing Around for a Clue

by Valerie Wolzien

A powerful sense of smell is one of the hallmarks of the golden retriever clans. Some say the golden's excellent nose is a result of a long-ago cross with an Irish setter; others say it was a co-mingling with bloodhounds that brought out the golden's formidable scenting prowess. It probably is a little of both, but whatever the reason, golden retrievers' remarkable sense of smell has led to their employment as cancer-detecting dogs, upland bird hunting dogs, bomb-sniffing dogs, and narcotics-detecting dogs, to name just a few of the breed's nasal-oriented tasks.

Something smells fishy to Susan Henshaw's golden retriever Clue in Valerie Wolzien's story. Wolzien is the author of more than a dozen mystery novels, almost all of which feature Connecticut homemaker Susan Henshaw, who often finds herself knee deep in a heaping pile of trouble. Wolzien's books include *Murder at the PTA Luncheon* (1988), *A Good Year for a Corpse* (1994), and *Remodeled to Death* (1995).

"Nosing Around for a Clue" first appeared in the anthology *Canine Crimes* (1998), edited by Jeffrey Marks.

The golden retriever is a natural in the water, and, amazingly, the golden can smell things under several feet of water. Photograph © Bill Marchel

"No one pays any attention. I sometimes feel like I'm a cipher in my own house. Oh, they expect me to do the shopping for them. And they'd all starve if I didn't cook. And entertaining . . . well, if I made just half of what a professional caterer would make on all the parties I've given, I'd be a rich woman, Clue. A rich woman."

Susan Henshaw, middle-aged suburban housewife, mother of two almost-grown-up children and wife of an advertising executive now busy at work in New York City, was spending the morning as she usually did on these warm June days. She was walking her dog in one of Hancock, Connecticut's, well-groomed parks.

"They don't even listen. No one. Not Jed, although I suppose that may just be the result of twenty-six years of marriage. Not Chad or Chrissy, of course, but what do you expect from a couple of kids in their twenties? Even Kathleen, my very best friend, seems to think I'm nuts this time. She says not to worry, that the answer will come to me. What sort of advice is that? Clue, you're the only one who gives me her complete attention."

The golden retriever looked up at Susan with love in her eyes. She was a great dog, Susan thought. A bit overweight, perhaps. Getting just slightly gray around her muzzle. As usual, she could use a good professional grooming. But she cared. And she listened. Oh, how she listened. And just now Susan needed a good listener. Just now she had to decide what to do with her life now that the kids were out of the house.

"It's called empty nest syndrome, Clue. And I had no idea what it meant. For years I've been laughing at the entire concept, telling everyone that I was dying to get the kids out of the house, that I would be happy to spend my days puttering around, reading, sleeping late, going to the Club and . . . and what, Clue? That's the problem. What did I think I was going to do with my time? With my life?"

They were circling a large pond. Clue, whose entire name was Susan Hasn't Got a Clue—a backhanded tribute to Susan's involvement in murder investigations—was walking sedately by Susan's side. The migrating geese were gone for the summer. The squirrels were apparently content to remain out of reach in the tops of the trees. And the only other dog walker in sight was a fabulously chic woman strolling beside her equally chic afghan hound.

"I hate to say it, Clue, but we look pretty dowdy compared to those two."

Clue didn't give a damn. A long line of young children, on a field trip with a local day care center, had appeared snaking across the horizon. Potential ball throwers, Clue seemed to think, pulling on her leash.

"No, Clue. They're busy. And their teacher wouldn't appreciate a hundred pounds of enthusiastic animal joining her group." She noticed that the afghan wasn't pulling away from her owner. "Be good, Clue!"

Oh, fine, now she was worrying about her dog's behavior the way she'd worried about that of her children when they were young. Clue,

Given the golden's powerful sense of smell, willingness to learn, and desire to please, the breed is a first-rate search-and-rescue dog. Photograph © Cheryl A. Ertelt

A patient pair along the California coast. Photograph © Sharon Eide/Elizabeth Flynn

ever aware of the changing environment, was now focusing on a large branch lying on the ground. Susan accepted the inevitable and allowed her dog to "retrieve" the branch.

Clue had never learned that picking up anything by one end would cause the other end to dangle—or, depending on its length, drag on the ground. Or, as in this particular case, smack into Susan's legs as they continued their walk around the pond.

The afghan hound and its owner were still trotting toward them. Susan was wondering just what would happen when the two dogs met when Clue dropped the stick, jerked the leash from Susan's hand, and ran into the pond.

Damn. She should have been prepared. Clue had been trying to get into the water every day for the last week or so. Now what the hell should she do? Beside, of course, jumping up and down on the edge of the water yelling for Clue to return.

"Your dog doesn't seem to be paying attention to you."

Naturally, this was the moment the afghan and its owner would reach her side.

"She . . . there must be something out there that she wants to retrieve," Susan was inspired to explain. "She is a retriever, you know."

"A very wet retriever."

Who would have thought it was possible? Even the afghan looked supercilious.

"My dog wouldn't have done that without a reason," Susan insisted stubbornly.

"Maybe." It was obvious the woman doubted it. "A friend of mine runs obedience classes. Perhaps you would like her phone number."

"I . . . I suppose so." Susan didn't want to admit that she and Clue had gone to dog training classes together one night a week for almost two years. Susan had learned that most other dogs were more obedient than her own. Clue had learned to sit, lie down, and stay—when she felt like it.

"We'll be here at this time tomorrow. Perhaps I can give you the information then."

"Yes. Yes. Thank you."

Clue was starting to swim back toward shore and Susan found herself alone. And then minutes later, she was soaking wet as Clue shook herself dry.

She picked up the dripping leash. "Let's go home, Clue."

The next day, Susan was late getting to the park. Her phone had been ringing all morning with news of the disappearance of a long-time resident of Hancock. Harriet MacHugh had moved to town as a young bride. After raising five children, she had become very active in volunteer work. Her executive abilities soon became apparent, however, and for over two decades she had run almost everything that needed running in town. Susan and Harriet had known each other for years and, when Harriet announced her retirement from volunteer work a few years ago, Susan

Bone or body down there? This golden will find out. Photograph © William H. Mullins

had organized a huge benefit dinner dance in Harriet's honor.

Two weeks ago, Harriet MacHugh had left her home in Florida saying goodbye to friends down there, telling them it was time she went home to Hancock. She had gotten off the plane in New York City that afternoon, flagged down a taxi, told the driver to take her to Connecticut, and disappeared.

Actually, Susan thought, absently scratching Clue's head, that was the story she had managed to piece together from six different phone calls. She was hoping to learn more when her friend Kathleen Gordon arrived. They were meeting to walk their dogs. Recently, Kathleen had succumbed to her children's desire for a puppy, so a small black Scottish terrier had become part of her household. Today was to be the puppy's first public appearance.

"And you're going to be good, aren't you, Clue?" Susan asked.

"Do you ever think maybe you spend too much time talking to that dog?" Kathleen had arrived.

"Wait until you've spent a little more time with Licorice, you'll end up talking to him, too."

"Maybe." Kathleen sounded as though she doubted it. "So what do you think about Harriet MacHugh? The rumor I heard at the grocery store this morning was that she was murdered."

"By who? Everyone in this town loved her."

"So I've heard. But, as an ex-police officer, I have to tell you, I find that a suspicious statement. No one is loved by everyone."

"Okay, and maybe love isn't the right word. But I do think most people in town respected her. Even my kids remember her as that kindly lady who always had a few Tootsie Rolls tucked in her purse to give away to children. If someone killed her, it was the cabdriver who claims to have driven her here from Kennedy Airport."

"Nope. Three separate people saw her here. Two even spoke to her. At least that's what I heard. Hey, there's Brett." Kathleen pointed to the good looking man who had just stepped out of a car, bearing the logo HANCOCK POLICE DEPARTMENT on its doors. "We can ask him all about it."

But Brett Fortesque, chief of the local police department, was the one asking questions.

"So, I don't suppose either of you saw Mrs. MacHugh here in the past few days?" he asked immediately after greeting them.

"Here? You mean in the park?"

"Not just here in the park, but right here beside this pond. We've found two other dog walkers who report seeing her early last week."

"Was she murdered?" Kathleen asked.

"There's no reason to think so. There's not much reason to think anything right now. The story, as I have it, is that she told her friends in Florida goodbye and that she was going to return to Hancock. Apparently everyone assumed she was going to fly back to Florida after a few days away and, when she didn't, people down there started to worry, called mutual friends up here, and apparently they hadn't seen her. That, coupled with the fact that she was certainly here, has got a lot of people worried."

"And?" Susan asked, as Clue drooled on her foot.

"And she was last seen standing fairly close to where we are now. Just looking out at the pond. Alone. Early in the evening exactly ten days ago."

"And no one has seen her since then?" Kathleen asked.

"Not that we can discover."

"Maybe she just saw what she wanted to see, got back in a cab, went to the airport, and flew to . . . to wherever she wanted to go next," Susan suggested. "Why are the police involved in this?"

"Her children are convinced that she came to Hancock for a pur-pose—something important."

"Any idea what?"

"Nope, but they're worried. They all say she wasn't a woman to do things casually and that she had been recently talking about a change in her life. All five of them have been ringing the phone off the hook down at the police station for the past few days."

"But you know how family can be—overly concerned," Kathleen sug-gested.

"Maybe, but—"

A wake in her path, a golden motors across a river. Photograph © William H. Mullins

"But Harriet's children include a congresswoman, a Pulitzer prize-winning journalist, a television talk show host, a Tony Award–winning actor, and a drummer for one of the most famous rock-and-roll bands in the country," Susan interrupted. She had lived in Hancock longer than her friend and had kept better track of its past citizens.

"Oh. I didn't know."

"So you can understand why we're particularly interested in finding out what happened to Harriet as quickly as possible."

Kathleen nodded, a serious expression on her face. "Nothing's worse than political pressure."

"Usually." Brett frowned. "But it's more than that. The truth is I really liked Harriet. She was . . . she is a very special woman. You all know what a fabulously affluent town Hancock is, but there are always citizens who are hurting—either financially or emotionally. What you probably don't know is that Harriet MacHugh endowed a discretionary fund that can be used to help these people. It's called the Mayor's Fund and there are a group of trustees who administer it. A lot of people have been helped with that money. And, as far as I know, none of them have had any idea where it came from."

"Really? I didn't know the MacHughs were particularly well off."

"They weren't. But she sold that big old Victorian she raised her family in for a large profit and moved into a very small apartment down in Florida. I understand she wanted her money to help people, rather than using it to keep her in a luxurious lifestyle."

"Good for Harriet." Susan was impressed. Here she was worrying about how to spend the last third of her life when this woman had simply decided to help others as much as possible with the resources she had. She would have said something about it if Clue hadn't suddenly taken it into her fuzzy little head to do a repeat of yesterday's impromptu swim.

"Clue! Come back! Now! Come, Clue!"

"Licorice! Licorice! Stop! Come back! Susan, he'll drown!" Kathleen joined her friend yelling for the two dogs to return to shore.

"You don't have to worry. It is natural for a dog to swim." The afghan's owner had joined them. Her dog, of course, sat sedately at her side, looking at the pond with disdain on her face.

"You see, the terrier is turning around."

Kathleen knelt down and flung her arms out. "Licorice. Come here, honey."

In a flurry of muddy water and fur, the Scottie ran out of the pond and into Kathleen's arms. Clue, as she had been the day before, was back in the middle of the pond, doing a fine example of the doggy paddle.

The afghan's owner was not impressed. "You might want to keep your puppy away from older, untrained dogs," she said to Kathleen. "Terriers are very impressionable, you know. And a bad influence early in life can create habits that are very, very difficult to break."

A happy and playful adolescent golden rests—for just a second—on the lawn. Photograph © Cheryl A. Ertelt

"Clue is not a bad influence! Clue is . . . she's a loving, sweet, kind . . . tell her, Kathleen, tell her what a wonderful dog Clue is!"

Kathleen was ineffectually trying to clean her puppy's head with a Kleenex. The task seemed to need her full attention.

Susan looked up at Brett. "Brett, tell her. Clue is a wonderful dog. All retrievers are like that. They . . . they retrieve things."

"What precisely is your dog retrieving now?"

"I don't know, but—"

"But it might be something important," Brett interrupted, grabbing the two-way radio that hung from his belt.

The three women exchanged looks. Kathleen and Susan had serious expressions on their faces. The afghan's owner seemed mystified. "If we're not needed here, Shalimar and I will just continue our walk," she announced. "We have a four-fifteen appointment with the hairdresser, don't we, sweetie?" Since no one objected to the plan, the elegant twosome continued their stately trek around the park.

"Do you think the same man does both dog hair and people hair?" Susan wondered aloud.

"Look, Susan, she's on her way back!" Kathleen cried, pointing to Clue.

"She always comes back. I have a pocket full of dog biscuits," Susan explained, standing up. "You all might want to be prepared to back up when she starts to shake off. . . . Brett? Did you hear me?"

Instead of moving away, Brett was walking toward the approaching dog. "Yeah, I heard you. Does Clue always swim around the same spot?"

"Sort of. I hadn't really thought about it. But, yes, I guess so."

"And she's been doing this every day since . . . since when?"

"She been trying to go in for days. Usually I manage to keep her with me."

"But how many days has she been trying to go in?"

"For the last seven . . . no, eight days."

"Are you sure about that?"

"Yeah. I brought her here after church a week ago Sunday, and that was eight days ago. She ran in then. I remember because I was wearing a new white linen skirt and it's at the cleaners now. She shook all over me then, too." Susan finished her statement as Clue repeated that particular gesture.

"Susan, could I borrow Clue this afternoon?"

"You want to borrow Clue? What for?"

Brett had finished mumbling into his two-way radio, and he flicked it shut and reached over for the dog. "I think Clue may know something we need to know," was all he would say, petting Clue's soaking wet head.

"You can have her for the afternoon, but, you know, you're getting wet." Susan pointed to where her dog was leaning against the police chief's leg.

"It doesn't matter. And if things turn out the way I think they will, I'll probably be getting a whole lot wetter."

*　*　*

In a field alive with smells, a tongue-lolling golden catches his breath. Photograph © Bill Buckley/The Green Agency

A line of trees circled the pond, around which bright yellow scene-of-the-crime tape was wound. A good number of citizens of Hancock, pausing in the middle of afternoon runs, jogs, walks, and strolls, were crowding about the tape. Susan and Kathleen sat on the hill where the daycare children had been tramping the day before. Kathleen's daughter, Emily, rolled around on the ground nearby with Licorice.

"So Brett asked you to stay away?" Kathleen was asking her friend.

"He thought I might be a distraction. You know, that Clue would pay more attention to me than to whatever is—might be—in the water."

"I've heard of this type of thing," Kathleen began, making sure her daughter was out of hearing before she continued. "As I understand it, the body has to be in a state of decay before it can be detected by the dog. And that's a dog which has been trained to find bodies. And I sure didn't know that anything could be detected under water."

"Brett called an expert from some sort of rescue group—this man trains goldens and German shepherds to find bodies, and he said that dogs can detect bodies under as much as thirty-five feet of still water. The pond is probably much shallower than that."

"But the body would have to have been down there long enough to decompose, right?"

"True. But if Harriet disappeared two weeks ago, her body might be . . . um . . ." She realized she was beginning to feel slightly ill. The thought of a body decomposing under water had been on the edge of her mind since Brett explained what he was going to do. Giving the body a name and a face was just a bit too much.

"I know what you're saying." Kathleen made it unnecessary for her to continue.

An aptly named road leads the way to this golden's home. Photograph © Sharon Eide/Elizabeth Flynn

"Brett said there was something else, but he didn't get a chance to tell me," Susan added, glaring at three trucks from local television stations parked so close to the crime-scene tape that the yellow ribbon bowed in toward the water. "Those vultures showed up and started shoving microphones in people's faces."

"If Harriet was murdered, it's news. Big news."

"Yes, but don't you think she would have hated this? I mean, if Harriet's down there, she certainly wouldn't have wanted all these cameras around when she . . . when she was pulled out," Susan said, starting to stand. "Do the divers have something? Do you see a . . . a . . ."

She didn't have to finish the question. What came out of the center of the pond, supported by three frogmen on loan from the Connecticut State Police department, was very obviously a body. A body dressed in a bright red flowered dress.

"So it was Harriet?"

"Yes. But she wasn't murdered. Brett says it was suicide."

That evening, Susan and Jed Henshaw were sitting together in a booth at the Hancock Inn, too upset to do more than pick at the wonderful meal on the table between them.

"How does he know that?"

"Apparently she sent a letter explaining her intentions to the lawyer who handled her financial affairs—unfortunately he was on vacation the week it arrived at his office. Since the letter was marked personal, it wasn't opened until he came back to the office this morning. His call came in to Brett's office while he was with the frogmen at the pond this afternoon."

"Did she say she was going to drown herself?" Jed asked.

"No, but it makes sense. The pond was named after her husband ages ago. Most people in town don't even know that."

"Or have forgotten it if they ever knew," Jed said. "Now that you mention it, I remember going to the dedication ceremony."

"Yes. That was years ago."

They picked at their food a bit longer and then gave up and ordered coffee and brandy.

"You know what I've been wondering?" Susan asked. "I've been wondering if I should still walk Clue in that part of the park."

"I don't think Harriet MacHugh would be happy if she thought she was keeping people away from one of the most charming spots in Hancock," her husband answered, reaching across the table to take his wife's hand in his.

It was three days later that Susan took her husband's good advice and returned to the path around the pond. The grass still bore evidence of being crushed by the crowd that had continued to mill around for over twenty-four hours after Harriet had been found. The tire tracks created by the television news vans had already been raked up and seeded by the

Impervious to the elements, a bear of a golden in snow up to his haunches. Photograph © Henry H. Holdsworth/Wild by Nature

Chelsea

by Peter C. Jones and Lisa MacDonald

Chelsea, a brave golden retriever, risked her life to save her master, Chris Dittmar, and a neighbor from two armed assailants. The men were chatting in the driveway with Chelsea at their feet when two strangers approached and asked the time. Seconds later, the two friends were staring down the barrels of a pair of loaded revolvers.

Terrified, neither man could utter a word. Suddenly, a deep-throated growl cut through the night air as Chelsea leapt toward the gunmen, her body outstretched and her mouth open wide. Dittmar was almost as shocked as the startled gunmen. "Because it was dark, all you could see was her white teeth."

Panicked, one of the assailants fired twice hitting Chelsea in the shoulder. Dittmar and his friend ran for cover while the second assailant aimed and fired. Bullets whizzed by as they bolted for the garage.

After the police arrived, Dittmar began a frantic search for Chelsea. Two blocks from home, she limped out from some bushes. "It was the happiest moment of my life," Dittmar said.

The fearless dog was rushed to an all-night animal clinic where she underwent surgery to remove the bullet. Chelsea was off her feet for three months, noise-shy for six, but is now fully recovered. She doesn't even walk with a limp.

Peter C. Jones and Lisa MacDonald are the authors of Hero Dogs: 100 True Stories of Daring Deeds *(1997), from which this story is taken. Chelsea was named the 1990 Ken-L Ration Dog of the Year for her bravery during this robbery attempt.*

The dedication of golden retrievers to their owners is legendary. Photograph © Bill Buckley/The Green Agency

efficient crews of the Hancock Parks Department. There were a few more walkers than usual, but other than these things, life had pretty much resumed its normal pace.

Until Clue dashed back into the water.

Susan and Jed were back at the inn, the evening of the same day, this time drinking glasses of white wine and laughing together.

"So Brett did the entire thing again. Hung the scene-of-the-crime tape? Called out the frogmen? Talked with reporters?"

"Yes. And there were even more people in the park this time. I think everyone in town had heard about it this time and then . . . and then . . ." Susan was laughing so hard she had to take a deep breath and a sip of wine before she could continue. "And then the frogmen came up to the surface with a red patent leather purse and Clue went nuts. I tried holding her. And one of the frogmen tried, too. Brett finally opened the purse and found a glob of chocolatey paper that had once been Tootsie Rolls and gave them to her. She swallowed them in one gulp and just sat down with this contented expression on her face. That's when all the cameras began to click. Clue's photograph may be on the front page of tomorrow's paper."

"Fabulous. Here's to Clue. A natural search-and-retrieve retriever if there ever was one."

"And, you know, I've been thinking. Maybe Clue found more than she was looking for in that pond," Susan said, suddenly serious. "Maybe she found a new career for both of us. The man who trains goldens said he would call in the next week or so. What do you think? Would that snotty woman with the well-groomed afghan be impressed if Clue and I became a professional search-and-rescue team?"

"Maybe." Jed's expression became more serious. "But I do know one thing. I know Harriet MacHugh would be glad to know that the Tootsie Rolls she always carried in her purse were appreciated even after her death. Who would have thought our dog would go back into the water for some water-soaked candy?"

"Anyone who knows her," Susan said, laughing. "Anyone who knows her."

Autumn color surrounding a golden in Idaho. Photograph © William H. Mullins

Willie

by Marilyn Weisbord and Kim Kachanoff, D.V.M.

The ability to detect an oncoming seizure before a person with epilepsy is even aware a seizure is imminent is a talent a select few golden retrievers possess. Goldens may achieve this remarkable feat of detection by using their sense of smell, though experts, to date, are unable to determine exactly how the dog is able to do this. But however they achieve this "sixth sense," the impact such a dog makes on the life of a person with epilepsy is nothing short of revolutionary. While going about the normal happenings of everyday life—climbing stairs, swimming, crossing streets—a person with epilepsy can feel safe and confident knowing the specially trained golden by his or her side will make quite a ruckus if a seizure is imminent. This willingness to offer a helping hand, so to speak, is another hallmark of the breed.

"Willie," the story of just such a seizure-sensing golden, originally appeared in *Dogs with Jobs: Working Dogs around the World* (2000) by Merrily Weisbord and Kim Kachanoff, a wonderful book filled with stories of remarkable dogs of all shapes, sizes, and missions. Weisbord is an award-winning writer, director, editor, and producer of Canadian film, television, and radio. She is also the author of four other nonfiction books and the winner of three Canada Council Awards for her nonfiction writing. Dr. Kim Kachanoff is a veterinarian in private practice in Canada.

A select few golden retrievers have the ability to detect an oncoming seizure in a person with epilepsy; Willie is such a dog. Photograph © Lon E. Lauber

JOANNE LEAVES WILLIE, her red-coated golden retriever, on the shore, and positions herself at the end of the pier. It's a hot July afternoon at Dog Scout camp, and men, women, children, and dogs of all shapes, colors, and sizes are swimming in the lake, sunning on the pebbly beach, or snoozing in the shade. Willie watches his sweet-faced blond mistress raise her camera, adjust the focus, and place her finger on the button to photograph the idyllic scene.

Then, like a thrown switch, something in Willie clicks.

He leaps to his feet and races toward Joanne, barking frantically.

Joanne heeds her dog's warning and lowers her camera. Willie nudges her insistently away from the edge of the pier. She heads quickly for solid ground. After five years together, she understands what he is signaling.

Within seconds, Joanne feels the strange aura, with its "sort of oniony smell," that precedes a grand mal seizure. The world begins to stretch and contract as if it's made of soft rubber, and Joanne collapses, unconscious.

Willie's special talent in predicting the onset of Joanne's epileptic seizures is one of the rarest, most mysterious canine gifts to humanity. Even in the specialized world of seizure dogs, trained to protect and help their epileptic owners, few possess Willie's uncanny ability to predict the onset of seizures. For Joanne, her dog's warnings mean the difference between a life of fearful worry and one of relative peace of mind.

At eight months of age, Willie received his basic training at Paws with a Cause in Wayland, Michigan, the largest service-dog training school in the United States. PAWS trains guide dogs, hearing dogs, mobility assistance dogs, emergency service dogs, and seizure dogs. Golden retrievers like Willie are a popular choice as a service dog. They were first bred in the British Isles in 1868 by Lord Tweedmouth, who crossed a Tweed water spaniel with a wavy-coated yellow retriever in an attempt to develop the perfect hunting dog. Further breeding over successive generations resulted in a water-loving golden retriever, which proved itself an excellent sporting dog, powerful and athletic, sound and well balanced. The breed's physical strengths and retrieving instincts, along with its sociability, self-confidence, and desire to please, are attributes inherent in Willie's gentle nature.

Michael Sapp, chief operating officer of Paws with a Cause, says it takes a special kind of animal to work as a seizure dog. Only two percent of the five hundred dogs tested so far have the necessary qualities of intelligence, patience, and gentleness required for seizure dog training. At PAWS, Willie learned to remove people with epilepsy from dangerous places at the onset of a seizure, and to protect them from harm while they were incapacitated. He was trained to operate emergency call devices for outside help, and respond to a buzzer, reminding his owner to take required medications. This training is vital to Joanne, because several times a day she has small petit mal seizures and blanks out briefly. With her conscious mind shut down, she might miss the buzzer and forget her medicine, thus precipitating a more severe grand mal seizure.

With a dogpack slung over her like saddlebags, this golden is ready to accompany and help her owner in any way she is needed.
Photograph © Henry H. Holdsworth/Wild by Nature

Going for a hike with a one-pup pack. Photograph © Henry H. Holdsworth/Wild by Nature

Of the twenty-eight seizure dogs trained at PAWS, only five showed Willie's remarkable ability to alert their owners to impending seizures. How they do it is still a mystery. Some researchers speculate that these dogs pick up a scent from the change in brain chemistry that accompanies a seizure. Or perhaps they detect tiny preseizure variants in the nervous system, like the seismic tremors that signal an earthquake. Whatever it is, the dogs that develop the talent do so only after spending years living with and caring for their owners. Their lifesaving seizure alerts are a wonder unequaled by human science. Before Willie arrived from Paws with a Cause, Joanne remembers a life filled with "fear and isolation." Going out alone with the specter of a grand mal seizure was potentially dangerous. People with epilepsy had been injured blacking out on busy streets. Some had awakened in hospitals listed as John or Jane Doe, robbed of all their identification and money. Joanne herself was once mugged while unconscious. Even in the relative security of her home during severe seizures, she was unable to summon help.

Now, Willie warns Joanne of impending seizures and protects her from harm, inside and out. When Joanne doesn't regain consciousness quickly enough after a seizure, he operates the footpad telephone her father built to call for help. "Willie," she says, "has given me my life back."

Because of his talent and unyielding devotion, Willie was named the Therapy Companion Animal of the Year by the Michigan Veterinary Medical Association. But in describing her six-year-old golden retriever, Joanne Weber uses much more personal terms: "Willie," she says, "is my savior."

On Call

Joanne wakes early to the chatter of chickadees outside the cabin window. She raises her sleepy head and sees Willie by the door, looking at her imploringly. Dog Scout camp shouldn't be wasted, his look implies. Let's get into the great outdoors.

The morning sun burnishes Willie's deep reddish fur to a golden hue as they amble down to the lake for a game of catch. Fellow campers poke their heads out of their rustic cabins, wave, and call greetings to Willie, as Joanne's artist's eye notes the play of light on his coat. She pats her dog's silky back. Knowing his mistress is safely surrounded by Dog Scout camp friends, Willie bounds ahead, only occasionally looking back.

Joanne watches the freedom of his movements, pleased to see her very responsible companion letting loose and enjoying camp. That's why she comes here—to join Willie in learning skills like flyball, backpacking, water rescue, Frisbee, search and rescue, and tracking, and to hear lectures on flora and fauna, wolf behavior, first aid, dog massage, and canine conditioning. But really, she comes so Willie can have fun with other dogs and relax.

They join a dozen happily chatting, sniffing dogs and people at a backpacking trail near the woods. The dogs, ranging from a small spaniel to a large Newfoundland, wear backpacks containing water bottles, bowls, flashlights, compasses, first-aid kits, pocketknives, extra leashes

Quinn: A Woman's Best Friend

by Celeste Mitchell

Sally Garland stands at a street corner in downtown Caldwell, New Jersey. She is listening to the flow of traffic. "Tammy? Are you with me?" she asks and reaches for her daughter's hand. "Yes, Mommy," answers the giggling first grader. Since Sally lost her vision seven years ago, the once-routine matters of everyday life—like crossing a busy street—are handled with extreme caution. And never without the guidance of a Seeing Eye dog named Quinn. As soon as Sally hears cars passing at her right, she knows the coast is clear. Following a hand motion and a verbal command, Quinn leads the way along the crosswalk. At the other side, a moment is spent hugging and kissing this very special dog. He deserves praise for a job well done. The whipping of his tail suggests he is just as pleased.

"Quinn takes his work very seriously," says the married mother of two. Tammy's brother, Jackson, is 8. "Our safety is his number-one priority and he has never let us down."

The even-tempered golden retriever is Sally's third guide dog (his predecessors have retired). The bond between Quinn and Sally is held together by a profound sense of loyalty. "When we walk together, it's as if we are one person," Sally explains. "He is like an extension of my left arm."

Which is exactly how this partnership is meant to be. "Sally is aware of where she is in time and space," says Carol Gray of The Seeing Eye, Inc., where Quinn was trained. "She directs the dog left, right or forward, and the dog decides if it is safe."

Sally begins her day at 6 A.M. in order to spend an hour of quality time with her canine companion. The kids sleep soundly as their mother gently brushes the dog's strawberry-blond coat. "It is Quinn's time," she says. Later, they head off to the supermarket for grocery shopping or to church, where Sally sings in the choir. As she makes her way around the town she has lived in all her life, people she knows—and some she doesn't—stop to say they admire her courage. The 44-year-old homemaker is the town's reluctant hero. She really sees herself as a regular person who cherishes independence just like everyone else. For Sally, running errands for her family is not boring or tedious. These are the fine details of a normal life.

You get the impression that if Quinn could talk, he would be equally modest. It is unlikely he would brag about the speed in which these two get around. In seven minutes they cover the four blocks from the Garlands' four-bedroom home to the grocery store. In contrast, traveling this distance with a white cane for the blind takes three times as long. And, Sally says, it is nerve-wracking. "A cane doesn't alert you to a hole in the sidewalk or a low-hanging branch that could scrape your face."

But Quinn's greatest gift by far is providing Sally with enough mobility to be an active mother. With Quinn at her left, Sally meets the school bus at the end of the driveway weekday afternoons. Twice a week she escorts Jackson and Tammy to their karate lessons. "I have been blessed with two healthy children," she says proudly. "I want to be there to cheer for them or wipe away the tears." Last year Sally signed on as the class mother to Jackson's second-grade class. She chaperoned field trips and organized bake sales. "I don't want my kids to feel different or left out."

This sensitivity is the outcome of her own experiences as a person with special needs. Born without vision in her left eye, she worked hard to adapt to a sighted world. And when her son was 5 years old, her right eye began to deteriorate. "I literally watched my vision disappear," Sally recalls. "It was scary." At 34, she teamed up with her first guide dog. She lost her vision completely just months before her daughter was born.

"At times it's hard, but I try to approach blindness as a challenge." she says. "I've learned a lot about life from Quinn. He takes things with such ease. He has given his whole life to me and expects only love and appreciation in return. Even now I marvel at how beautifully it works."

Celeste Mitchell is a former writer and editor for Family Circle *magazine.*

A guide golden retriever and her owner cross a busy street. Photograph courtesy of The Seeing Eye.

and collars, and, of course, pooper-scoopers. The morning's hike is a five-miler through the forested hills. The training purpose of the hike is to build up and maintain the dog's conditioning, especially necessary for service dogs like Willie, who tote their owners' valuables and medications wherever they go. The camp's motto for dogs is "Let us learn new things, that we may become more helpful" and the motto for their owners is "Our dogs' lives are much shorter than our own, so let's help them enjoy their time with us as much as we can." But the real reward for the dogs is simply a great walk in the woods in the company of their owners and a pack of canine playmates.

The group strolls at an easy pace, giving the dogs time to explore. Even on these camp hikes, Willie feels obliged to remain on call. He is far up the trail when he hears the sound of Joanne's buzzer, but his reaction is immediate. He wheels around and bounds toward her with his alarm bark. "It's okay, Willie," she reassures him as she takes her medication. "Go have some fun."

The dog and human hikers climb to the peak of the hillside overlooking the lake and the camp below. Satisfied that Joanne has taken her medication, Willie and a frisky cocker spaniel circle a chattering treed squirrel, their faces marked by the indignant look dogs get when confronted by small, noisy, inaccessible rodents. Finally, they give up, moving on to easier prey—a birch branch at the base of the tree. Willie, the retriever, happily grasps the wood treasure in his mouth, prances and dances around the scampering spaniel, shakes the stick vigorously, flips it in the air, and pounces before it hits the ground.

Lonnie Olson founded the Dog Scouts of America camp when she saw the sheer joy in her Border collie's eyes as he played on the lakeshore with other dogs. The only existing camps she knew focused on formal obedience, and she envisaged a more playful learning experience. Joanne knows this camp was conceived for dogs, but she admits she has come to enjoy these camp weeks as much as Willie does.

Two hours later, the weary and relaxed hiking crew arrives back at the camp for water rescue training. The heat has been building all morning and people and dogs jump gratefully into the refreshing lake to practice lifesaving. Willie fetches Joanne a life jacket, then a rescue rope, and, finally, himself as a furry flotation device. Joanne clutches his back, feeling the water eddy around her body, laughing to see the lake churning with lifesaving dogs and because she feels so good. Willie pulls her safely to shore. Then he shakes great arcs of spray over everyone and bounds back into the shallows, a true water-loving retriever.

Joanne's dog painting class begins soon after lunch. The Dog Scout campers are fitted with sponge booties dipped in nontoxic water-soluble paint, and the room gears up for a wildly hilarious art session. Owners hold up cardboard canvases and move them around while the dogs happily flail away, getting half the paint on the cardboard canvas and half on themselves and their laughing masters. After each successful swipe, the dogs are given a treat, which encourages their artistic endeavors. Willie has more practice than the others, since his painting lessons began in Joanne's studio, where she noticed Willie's curiosity about her painting.

A golden raising its head for praise from its owner. From the original pencil sketch by Christopher S. Smith. Reprinted by permission of the artist.

A drippy and disheveled golden in a crystal-clear California lake. Photograph © Sharon Eide/Elizabeth Flynn

Willie already knew how to "wave," or lift his paw in the air. It was a short step from there to taping a paintbrush to his paw, holding up a piece of cardboard, and letting him go at it. Now, Willie is something of an expert, and his paintings are auctioned off at charity fund-raisers. Willie whacks the canvas with a gleeful look in Joanne's direction. It is one of his habits to look directly at her, eye to eye. "You're a good boy, Willie," she says. His wonderful red coat is speckled with green and yellow paint and he sports what looks very much like a grin on his face.

Before supper, everyone heads back to the lake for a final swim and to wash off the body paint. Joanne carries her camera to record the beach scene as a memento. Willie waits dutifully on shore, watching her walk to the end of the pier. She adjusts the focus and clearly sees her fellow campers scrubbing off paint and Willie, stretched out comfortably on the beach, gazing back at her through the lens.

King of the haystack, a laid-back golden relaxes on his domain. Photograph © Sharon Eide/Elizabeth Flynn

Suddenly, Willie's entire demeanor undergoes a dramatic shift. He senses in Joanne an intangible signal so slight that only he, in all the world, can perceive it. He takes off toward Joanne like a shot, barking as if his lungs will burst, pleading with her to get off the dock before the seizure strikes.

When Joanne first hears him, she is surprised by the warning because she can honestly say, at that moment, surrounded by friends on this beautiful July afternoon, she has never felt better. But then comes the smell of onions, and the world begins to pitch and weave. She makes it to solid ground and settles in, still conscious, but her brain has lost control of her limbs and speech. The seizure builds inexorably toward its height. There is a pulsing strobe effect, without the light. Electrical impulses fire wildly in her brain, and she convulses helplessly on the ground. Gradually, she loses consciousness. The last thing she sees is Willie standing over her, his eyes dark with concern, protecting her with his body. Then there is nothing.

Willie hovers over her. As always, he tries to revive her by licking her face. Joanne's friends crowd around, grateful to Willie for averting potential danger. If the seizure had struck unexpectedly, Joanne might have pitched into the water, hit her head, and drowned.

Finally, Joanne opens her eyes. The first thing she sees is Willie, her friend and protector, looking anxious. He is waiting for her to say the reassuring words, "I'm okay, Willie, I'm okay."

* * *

Back in their condo in Grand Blanc, Michigan, Willie settles into his favorite place. From the settee beside the studio window, he keeps an ear cocked for Joanne and checks to make sure all is well in the outside world. Joanne is immersed in fine-tuning an illustration program on her computer. Because her seizures are made much worse by stress, she avoids high-pressure commercial deadlines, but enjoys a wide range of graphic and fine-arts work. Willie recognizes an elderly couple from next door and gives them a wag. A squirrel scampers across the lawn and his face looks momentarily indignant. But he doesn't bark. That's saved for when it matters.

When Joanne takes a break to do laundry, Willie scampers down to be by her side. She recently had back surgery and has trouble lifting the hamper. With no prompting, Willie drags the hamper from her bedroom to the laundry room. He is halfway down the hall when the phone rings. He stops and looks at Joanne with a "You-want-me-to-get-it?" look.

Joanne smiles. "It's okay, Willie," she says. "I'll get it." Willie can fetch the portable phone and often does, but she worries sometimes that Willie is too devoted, too responsible. That's the beauty of Dog Scout camp, she thinks—hikes, water, play, some fun in Willie's life.

The buzzer goes off and Willie barks his medication bark, not letting up until he sees Joanne take her pills. Then he's quiet. The golden dog stretches out on his back on the settee, all four paws in the air, head upside down, mouth drooping, and long tongue hanging out. Joanne glances up from her computer and smiles. Sensing her looking at him, the upside-down Therapy Companion Animal of the Year thumps his tail and wriggles impishly. Joanne can't help getting up to rub his belly and Willie closes his eyes in bliss. Both rest securely, knowing the other's care and devotion is total and unqualified. Moments later, Joanne hears her big dog snoring.

For Joanne, even a sleeping, noisily reverberating Willie is comforting. He is at her side, ready to help if she needs him. She thinks of the good times, and the times that aren't so bad because Willie is there to look out for her. She wants to hug him. She begins to say, "You're a good boy, Willie," then decides to keep quiet, to let him sleep.

Golden and owner on a walk in the Canadian wilderness. Photograph © Johan Adlercreutz

Joe's World

by Muriel Dobbin

Another quality of golden retrievers is loyalty, including a passionate desire to look out for their owners and protect them from harm. That look of concern on your golden's face when she perceives trouble and her willingness to spring to action if trouble gets out of hand are other ways a golden retriever offers a helping hand.

Scottish-born reporter and author Muriel Dobbin spins a hilarious and unconventional tale of just such a golden retriever. The golden has great concern for his owner, with whom he shares a deep bond. Liberally employing the license fiction allows, Dobbin describes this bond from the viewpoint of the golden himself—a dog with the ability to write down his thoughts and who also enjoys regular imbibing of spirits.

Dobbin is the author of several books including *A Taste for Power* (1980), *Going Live* (1987), and *Going Public* (1991). "Joe's World" first appeared in Dobbin's 1983 book of the same name.

A contemplative golden under the setting sun. Photograph © Lon E. Lauber

IT ISN'T THAT I don't like him, but I've had to get rid of them before. They always seem to feel it's their duty to rescue her from her lifestyle, and since a lot of her life is centered around me, that is worrying. First they think She drinks too much and then they cause trouble because I like a martini or two at the end of the day myself. Or in the middle of it, depending on whether it's raining. How can you let that dog drink? they ask her, and She is a little embarrassed about the fact that She and I have been drinking together pretty much since I was a pup. She was a cub reporter then, and not flying around on big assignments the way She is now.

She used to defend me. He doesn't drink much, She would say. But since Charlie more or less moved in, it's been different. Charlie and I got along pretty well for a bit. He didn't disapprove of my drinking. But he made fun of it, which to my mind was worse. I used to think he invited people over just to watch me lap up a little gin, and they would all sit around shrieking with laughter. She knew I was embarrassed. I have always prided myself on my dignity, so She must have known I was embarrassed, even if I was the star of their parties. Half of them laughed themselves sick, and the rest just threatened to call the S.P.C.A. They were generally the ones who sniffed and said dogs don't drink.

Well, generally speaking, dogs don't drink, but most dogs don't have my problems. I mean, I have to look out for someone who, in my opinion, really can't take proper care of herself.

Many's the night She's cried until my fur was so wet I thought I'd get pneumonia, or at least rheumatism. And when She isn't home, which is a lot of the time, I get lonesome enough to have a small drink by myself in the shank of the evening, as they say. I seem to spend a lot of time watching her pack to fly off somewhere in one of those campaign planes She laughs about with her friends when She's at home. It was one of those times She was away that I began playing with her typewriter. I used to watch her pounding away at it, and it didn't look too difficult, especially once I figured out you had to push a button to start it. So I practiced a bit and it passed the time. Then I began putting things down. I mean, when I read some of the stuff She writes, not to mention some of her friends, the kind of thing I run into makes a lot more sense, at least in my world, which I consider a much more peaceful place than hers, because it deals with problems that are simple but not silly.

I must admit I do like the times when She's at home. I like listening to her and I think She likes talking to me. I like the sound of her voice, although I wish She wouldn't talk baby talk to me. She has a soft voice and She doesn't often shout, and She hardly ever cries because She knows it troubles me. There was a time one of the men She brought home made her cry and I bit him. It seemed like the thing to do at the time, and the way She hugged me after he went slamming out, I knew She was pretty pleased about it. We finished off the martinis together that night.

I think that's what disturbs me about this thing with Charlie. I haven't had any trouble getting rid of the others, and She's always seemed glad of it. But with Charlie, it's been different. She met Charlie just after She

Hanging out on the couch with chew toy at the ready. Photograph © William H. Mullins

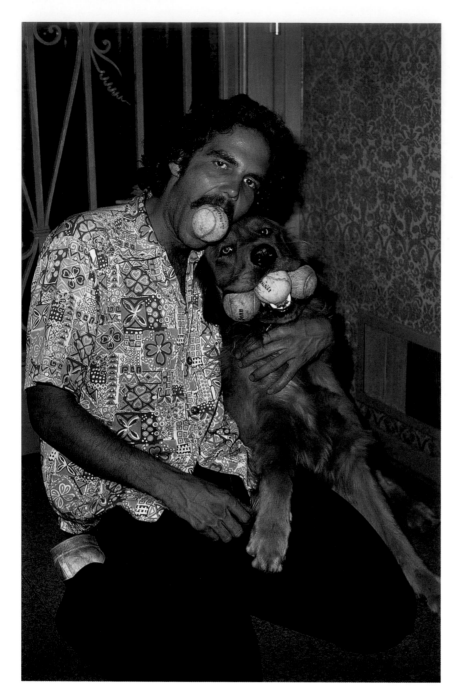

Mouthfuls of tennis balls for golden and owner alike. Photograph © Diane Ensign/The Green Agency

broke up with Tim, and I have to admit, by comparison, Charlie was an immense improvement. Tim was thirty-four going on fourteen, and a member of that breed who say they love a woman who is liberated, then sulk when she doesn't do the laundry. He kept explaining to her how sensitive he was, and he criticized her all the time for not realizing how She was denting his sensitivities. By the time I decided the moment was right to dent something else, She was a walking mass of guilt. And as he left, he accused her of putting me up to biting him in what I have to say was a sensitive spot. She cried into her martinis until the vermouth turned to salt, and I was actually grateful when a week later She came home and said She had met somebody who was a lawyer and who took care of her.

I should have been warned by that phrase, because She'd always relied on me to take care of her. But Charlie was nice to her. He didn't want her to take care of him, that was true, although it seemed to be mostly because he didn't think anybody could do anything better than he could. But he made a great fuss over her, and he had the sense to make a great fuss over me. That was before he discovered we drank together, and then he started braying like a donkey about my capacity for gin. When She laughed, just a little, along with him, I knew I was in for trouble. And I didn't have any excuse to bite him; I consider violence a tactic of last resort.

Charlie obviously is going to require a more subtle strategy, and I try not to think about what will happen if that doesn't work. She talks about him as if he's always going to be with us, and won't that be nice? I deliberately do not wag my tail, but She's so besotted about him, I don't know if She notices as much as She usually does. I'm cool toward him, of course, but he is so all over her that She doesn't notice that either. Once or twice he's tried to close the door in my face, but I took care of that. I sulked so much when he suggested that maybe I should go to obedience school—at my age?—they almost had their first fight. Unfortunately, he's a fast learner, and he never picked on me again.

I think the worst thing is that he occupies so much of her time. She doesn't have much time left over from her job, anyway, so I practically don't see her any more. She's out with him right now, and even if She does come home, which She doesn't always, he'll probably be with her, which means She and I can't be cozy the way we used to. It's funny how much it annoys me that he laughs at my drinking, because She used to sort of giggle, but that was different. And She might not have giggled either if she'd known how much I drank, because it costs her a lot more than Bonzo's Munch Bones.

We've been together a long time and, as you can probably tell, I'm very fond of her, although I can't understand why anyone would get paid for wandering around writing down the silly things other people say.

But, She does get paid, and we live in a nice house with plenty to eat for both of us and almost enough gin. It's sort of a town house, I think they call it, and it has a nice backyard with a big shady tree and roses that climb up the fence so I can sniff them when I'm napping on a hot afternoon. There are other town houses in this complex, which has a swimming pool and a lot of grass and places to wander. And a lot of the other residents also are sensible enough to have animals, even if some of them are cats.

For example, there is my cousin Joseph, who lives three doors away, and is older than me. His mission in life, apart from sleeping, is giving advice to other golden retrievers. He says other dogs don't count because they don't have our distinguished ancestry. I'm not averse to compliments on my lineage, of course, but I must say I've encountered a number of remarkably dense dogs of my own breed. Like Gracie, who had trouble telling up from down when it came to stairs and who once got banned from a friend's home because she helped him eat the sofa. Or Dickens, who swallowed several brass padlocks, more or less because he couldn't think of anything else to do with them. Or Tyler, whose passion for pursuing cars almost caused him to need a tail implant.

And of course when you get to other breeds, it gets worse. I mean, there's Alfred P. Quagmire, an exotic but energetic white creature, who looks like he was knitted. No golden retriever I know would have taken on a bottle of glue, although a pup I know called Gusty did try to eat his own bed until he found it was filled with woodchips. And a friend called Taffy conducts an unending war with flower pots, which she considers a version of the MX.

Anyway, at least in my world we can tell a golden retriever from a cocker spaniel, which is more than I can say for the magazine editors who printed a photograph of Vice President Bush and his wife with their golden retriever C. Fred Bush. C. Fred, as far as I could tell, was unquestionably a cocker spaniel, and nobody ever suggested that by night all dogs were gray. But that does lead me to my grievance that in the literary world, at least, dogs seem to be taking a second place to cats.

I believe dogs have been done an injustice in terms of public recognition, which was another reason I began this journal. For example, I find reading the bestseller list of the *New York Times* book review section downright discouraging. What is this national passion with cats? The only memorable thing I know about cats is that the ancient Egyptians used to shave off their eyebrows when their cat died. But I seriously doubt that was the kind of animal who would do a sort of frozen samba on television, which is the kind of thing animals stoop to nowadays to keep their owners in cash.

I know a couple of cats in my neighborhood who seem pretty normal. Like Terminal Hate down the block; there's a cat who despises the world, and just about anybody would respect him. Rhinestone Cowcat is a pretty tough little cookie, too, in spite of that silly collar her owner puts around her neck. But Joseph and I have been wondering whatever happened to dogs? I mean, you can still see those old Rin Tin Tin and Lassie movies on late-night television. Those were dogs in the true tradition of man's best friend. Not that I have anything against Benji or Old Yeller or Big Red, but I had a severe case of the heaves over that mechanical animal, Chomps, that Hollywood came up with. You would think there were enough good dogs out of work without their concocting something made of foam rubber and imported fur.

She's told me about political dogs She has known, and I wouldn't care for that kind of a dog's life. Roosevelt's Fala, from what I have read, seemed like a decent, down-to-earth Scottie, and Bobby Kennedy's Brumas and Freckles were fairly normal animals who got away with disgracing themselves in fancy restaurants. But those beagles who belonged to LBJ, they had my sympathy. In addition to being saddled with those idiotic names—what self-respecting dog could go through life answering to "Here, Her! Here, Him!"—they had to submit to being picked up by their ears. Anyone who picked me up by the ears would get molars in his wrist, Secret Service or no Secret Service. Then there was Johnson's collie, Blanco, the one She told me was so nervous it had to be given tranquilizers, or "gentlers," as its owner called them. It was probably a good deal too gentle to be taken on walks with fifty flat-footed reporters tripping on its back paws. Very unnerving!

But this cat fad is typical of the kind of thing people do. They have so little perception of what lies beyond the narrow boundaries of their own noses. For example, She says She knows I understand every word She says, and sometimes She thinks I'm about to talk back to her. But as I said to Joseph, why should I talk back to her? What would I say that She would understand? Would any of them understand my world, where there are no hours or schedules or trains and planes and buses, where there are only the passing of time, and the birds and bugs and mice, and even cats.

This is the world that has always been, a world where there is always time to do something really important, like stop and talk to a melancholy mouse or watch the sunlight fall on the foliage of an oak tree, or smell the fragrance of roses in wet grass. The only time people care about sunlight is when they're out by their pools, turning themselves peculiar and violent shades of red. They never seem to take time to sit and watch quietly, and I think that's because they're afraid to be alone. They carry

Shaking the water off at the end of a long day at the lake. Photograph © Bill Marchel

their noise with them in those ugly boxes that make it impossible to hear rain on the roof. And the sad part is, you can learn a lot just lying in the grass waiting for an interesting bug to come along. Children know that, but adults are too stupid to remember it, which is why so many children grow up seeing nothing but the television screen, which is the equivalent of growing up inside a kaleidoscope full of violent color and movement, meaning nothing.

She likes to watch old movies on television, which was how I came to know about the dog films. And we've had a few good laughs over animal commercials. She says that whenever I see a dog in one of those ridiculous advertisements, I whiffle, which I suppose is a good enough term for what I consider a dignified, if gruff, chuckle. Cats don't think those commercials are funny, but they know there's money in them. Perhaps one of the reasons cats are so popular these days is that they are in tune with the selfishness of the age.

Most cats I know are pragmatists and proud of it. Dogs are the only idealists left in the world, and if you don't believe me, just think of the way a dog owner is greeted when he comes home and then compare that scene to the homecoming of a cat owner. The dog owner walks through the door and the dog is bounding up, tail wagging, eyes shining, ears perked, just vibrating with eagerness to bring slippers, carry the paper, lick a hand, fix a drink.

The cat owner walks in and the cat raises its head languidly from the best armchair and says, you're late, where's my dinner, am I expected to

A portrait of a golden retriever in her element. From the original oil painting by Robert K. Abbett. Reprinted by permission of the artist.

wait around and starve while you're out slopping it up in some disgusting bar? Intimidated, the cat owner rushes to the kitchen without taking his coat off, opens a can, mixes things up, freshens the water in the cat dish, all the while making nauseating mewing sounds to ingratiate himself with His Majesty, who is still curled up in the living room and may or may not emit a perfunctory purr in response to all this attention.

The devoted dog-next-door will, of course, wait patiently for his dinner while the owner has a drink or two, reads the paper, and considers his own menu for the evening. Some dogs forget their manners and get rude when their stomachs have rumbled enough. But a well-trained dog owner requires only the merest nudge of a reminder. Just enough to knock the newspaper out of his hand will do it, I have found.

Nobody seems to realize that when you look into a cat's eyes, what you're seeing is usually pure contempt. I watch people fawning over Terminal Hate, and I know he's barely restraining himself from laying their wristbones bare. He's done that once or twice, but of course he was forgiven. Dogs bite only for good reason; they're remarkably patient about having their ears rubbed the wrong way or having to sit and listen to nonsense. A cat's expression tends to discourage nonsense.

Even Joseph was complaining the other day about the amount of time his owners spend worrying about their electricity bills. He kept wondering why they didn't just build a fire or put on a sweater and think about something more useful. That's significant, because Joseph isn't always too alert. He has never left our world, and he says a lot of my restlessness is a result of the fact that I keep putting at least one paw over the doorstep into the world of people, which would depress any dog. I found this a remarkably astute statement coming from Joseph because, although he is a relative and I am fond of him, I have to suspect that if you picked up one of his ear flaps, you might see clear through to the other side of his head.

Joseph is not exactly retarded, but I think that affair his mother had with an over-the-hill boxer diminished his natural intelligence. As he said rather cynically once, his mother was known in the neighborhood as Terminal Heat. And Joseph is the only dog I know who can't remember why he's standing beside a tree with one leg raised.

Perhaps Joseph's charm lies in his capacity for self-containment and contentment. I have rarely known him to be ruffled, even when poked by small children. He avoids looking at newspapers and the only thing I have ever seen him read is Henry James, which he said he found edifying without being disruptive to the soul. For myself, I prefer Thurber. There was a man who understood dogs. There was nothing cute about Thurber's animals; he treated them like adults and that's how they acted. I think a lot of decent dogs have been corrupted nowadays. The worst of them have begun to act like people and that's a sad state of affairs for a dog. I believe it was Thurber who said man was trying to drag dogs down to his level, and he may have been right.

Joseph says I spend too much time worrying about people, but the thing is, I feel sorry for them because they miss so much. They move so fast they rarely see anything, and if they do, unless it has a designer label on it, they don't want it. They don't seem to realize that a lot of things haven't changed for a very long time and, well . . . take buttercups; they are just what they seem to be, no better and no worse, and that's probably how it's supposed to be. Not even kings or presidents or politicians have managed to change that. Mine is a world where buttercups are important, and one of the reasons I am fond of her is that I think She has a glimmering of that.

In a sense, I consider her a subject for research. Her world doesn't make much sense to me, and mine is probably as much of a mystery to her. I suppose that's why I finally decided to make use of my new typing skill and put down, for whomever may one day read it, this glimpse of a world where people have no place, not only because they have lost sight of that world but, sadly, because they have lost their place in it. It is certainly a world without politicians, whom I do not consider people. She was writing a long story the other day analyzing the election chances of a presidential candidate who seems to me to be on the intellectual level of Rhinestone Cowcat, a dingbat of a cat if ever there was one. To be candid, I have lost the ability to tell one politician from another. I can understand that they all want the same thing. What I can't understand is why they all sound alike. Most political speeches should be chopped up and sold as sedatives.

Joseph listened to a lengthy political speech once, and slept so long afterward, his owners called the vet. But I understood his reaction. Although I have more curiosity about people than Joseph, I find myself nodding off whenever somebody stands up and declares himself dedicated to doing good for mankind instead of coming right out and admitting he can't wait to get his paws on all those perks that go with holding office, and that he's just drooling for the junkets and joy rides—not to mention the groupies—and don't let anyone tell me he would faint dead away at the thought of a little comfy corruption to pad his bank account.

Politics is entertaining, of course, and not quite as violent as the movies, but nobody ever seems to admit he's running because he's desperate to boss people around and never mind all this malarkey about saving his fellow citizens. Most of them have a lot in common with those religious fellows, who seem to feel they've cornered the market on salvation.

My paw is getting tired, so I think I'll stop and put my journal away under the refrigerator, which is convenient to the gin, and anyway She never cleans under there. Which reminds me, She's running low on gin, and I expect She and Charlie will finish what's left of it if they do come home. It's getting late, so maybe She'll stay over at his place again, which I suppose means I can finish the gin myself, but on the other hand, I don't want him snickering at me again when they find the empty bottle. And of course it would be a good deal more embarrassing to have them find me typing. If he thinks it's funny that a dog drinks, he might laugh himself into a heart attack over a dog keeping a journal. Which may be something I should keep in mind, the way things are going.

Facing page: *Cute on just about every level imaginable, a fluffy golden pup poses for pictures in a wooden box. Photograph © Sharon Eide/Elizabeth Flynn*
Overleaf: *The golden gallop—a happy, loping gate—is readily displayed during a game of fetch. Photograph © Daniel Dempster*

Part IV:

The Soul of the Golden Retriever

"Canute was a male golden retriever we had acquired as a puppy when the children were still a tumbling, preteen pack. Endlessly amiable, . . . he suffered all . . . as if life were a steady hail of blessings."
John Updike, *Trust Me. Short Stories,* 1987

Left: *Crystals of snow on his whiskers and face, a golden warms himself under a wintertime sun. Photograph © Lon E. Lauber*
Above: *A nearly white golden and her twelve-year-old owner. Photograph © Lynn M. Stone*

The Honorary Huichol

~

by Charles Kulander

People and golden retrievers are soul mates, creatures meant to be together. And the soul of the golden resides in a happy and playful place, filled with an unquenchable desire to bond with and to help humankind. Humans, often despite great efforts to the contrary, can't help but be caught up in a golden retriever's enthusiasm and dedication.

Of course, some goldens, though happy and playful like the rest of their clans, cause a considerable amount of chaos just being themselves. Charles Kulander has had plenty of first-hand experience with a golden of this ilk through Boojum, his family's golden. Kulander is a former managing editor of the *Mexico City News* and *Baja California* magazine, and he is now a Utah-based freelance travel writer. His work has been published widely in newspapers and magazines in the western United States, and he is also the author of *West Mexico: From Sea to Sierra* (1992).

"The Honorary Huichol" first appeared in the anthology *Travelers' Tales: A Dog's World* (1998), edited by Christine Hunsicker.

A portrait of a perfectly groomed, gorgeous golden may mask a deep-seated tendency to cause chaos whenever possible. Photograph © Sharon Eide/Elizabeth Flynn

"YOU'RE GOOFING OFF while I'm out there working like a dog." We were leaving in less than two hours to visit the most mysterious tribe of Indians on the continent and there they were, watching an *I Love Lucy* rerun.

"Dad," said Olivia, my ten-year-old daughter. "Have you ever seen a dog work?"

She had a point. Boojum, our golden retriever—actually she's more of a dishwater blond—was lying on the bed fast asleep. She was our watchdog, which meant that you could watch this dog do nothing all day long, except occasionally bark at odd phenomena. Like our next-door neighbors.

Do dogs work? I guess it depends on the breed. Each has its own special characteristic. Chihuahuas have a Napoleon complex, German shepherds are into sado-masochism, and wolf hybrids, if given the chance, will eat their owners. Golden retrievers are the Bleeding Hearts of the dog world, overly sensitive, insecure, and wanting to be everybody's best friend. I've seen golden retrievers work as sniffer dogs at international airports. They catch drug smugglers by wagging their tails furiously.

Boojum was our designated guard dog on this trip. I had been training her in defensive attack techniques using my daughter's dolls as assailants. I wasn't sure how she would react to real criminals, but she'd do quite well if we were ever attacked by a renegade band of Cabbage Patch dolls.

Boojum will have her moment, I told myself as we drove down Mexico's Highway 15 on our way to Tepic. Then she will rise to the challenge. The climate turned hot the farther south we drove, and Boojum's only apparent challenge so far was to find a place to soak, such as in the puddles of oil found at most Pemex gas stations.

At a trailer park in Guaymas, a gardener came running into our camp, gesturing towards the swimming pool.

"*No es sanitario,*" he muttered angrily. We ran to the pool, where Boojum was paddling about like the Exxon Valdez, leaving behind her own personal oil slick.

In Mazatlán, Boojum had a chance to redeem herself. After leaving the bank, I noticed the van had a flat. A sports car pulled up alongside, and the driver offered his help. My wife fairly leaped out of the van. In Mexico, she is always looking for a public opportunity to show how a woman can do anything a man can. Jacking up a van was the perfect political act. After the sports car zoomed off, I searched for the cause of the flat. Knife puncture. At the same time, Jil yelled that her purse was missing. The man in the sports car had an accomplice who reached in the front window to grab Jil's purse while she was busy jacking up the car. Dashiel and Livi had been absorbed in their Game Boy. Our only witness was Boojum, who was sitting where the purse had been. This was her moment, I fumed. And what did she do? She did what all golden retrievers are trained to do. She wagged her damn tail.

By the time we reached the Tepic airport, we decided to board her with a local veterinarian while we flew up to visit the Huichol Indians. Big mistake taking a dog on a trip like this, I complained. But the

A snowstorm in the Tetons and a bear of a golden. Photograph © Henry H. Holdsworth/Wild by Nature

Practicing short retrieves in a no-longer-suitable-for-bubble-baths tub in the backyard. Photograph © Sharon Eide/Elizabeth Flynn

vintage DC-3 that flies up to the sierras was already loading for an early departure. The next flight was in three days. We'd have to take the dog.

"Does she bite?" the pilot asked me, nudging her with his foot.

"I wish."

The almost inaccessible mountains of Jalisco and Nayarit appeared disconcertingly close as the overloaded plane droned through the canyons. These craggy peaks have protected the Huichol for centuries, one of the last tribes in Mexico still holding to unadulterated pre-Hispanic beliefs. The passengers were going home for the ceremonies dressed in a psychedelic array of yarn, beads, and feathers, each tassel and design wrought with personal religious symbolism. They didn't pay much attention to us—we came from the same factory as our Levis—but they were curious about Boojum, who lay sprawled out in the aisle, still depressed from her Mazatlán scolding.

The plane bounced hard on the dirt runway, spun around on one engine, and came to a halt in front of a tiny village of adobe huts. We stepped down the gangway and into a crowd of Huichol, who aren't known for greeting strangers but instead stand back with arms crossed, examining you as if you were just another cardboard box coming off the plane. That is, until Boojum bounded down the stairs. They all stepped back in fear and surprise.

A Huichol family allowed us to pitch our dome tent near their rancho, in a grove of pine trees scented with wood smoke. After setting up camp, Jil and I left to pay our respects to the head shaman, the high priest of

Huichol theology. The Huichol have their own gods and spirits based on a holy trinity of deer, corn, and peyote. The deer is a particularly holy animal. Peyote grows in its footsteps, and visions are transmitted through the antlers, like an antenna to the God Channel. But deer are scarce in Huichol land, almost extinct, and if you could judge by their tiny prongs, antenna reception had been getting progressively weaker.

Before leaving on our trip, Boojum had dragged home an enormous deer antler from a neighbor who had just returned from a successful hunt. After scolding Boojum, we returned the antler, but the next morning—the day we were leaving for Mexico—the antler was back on our porch, while Boojum lurked in the bushes, her head hung low.

"This is destiny," I told Jil, as I packed the antler into the van.

"Looks like petty theft to me," she said.

Jil and I took the huge deer antler to the *caliguey,* a ceremonial structure similar to a Hopi's *kiva.* The shamans were gathered here to celebrate the return of the *peyoteros,* who had just come back from their annual 200-mile pilgrimage to harvest peyote in the San Luis Potosi desert. We were invited inside. Images slowly formed as our eyes adjusted to the orbs of candlelight. Prayer sticks and beaded gourds lay on an altar, along with miniature god chairs and tiny antlers. Men were talking to themselves, lost in a peyote trance, coughing and spitting on the ground. Women pit-patted tortillas while dogs scavenged the ground, fighting over scraps. Presiding over this scene was the head shaman, reclining like Solomon on his throne. We approached quietly, and gave him the antler.

We told him the story of how our dog had brought it home, and that it was our humble offering from the land of Utah. He nodded his approval, and within minutes it was ribboned with prayer sticks and placed alongside the other sacred objects on the altar.

Thinking we had paid the proper respect for admission, the next morning we entered the village with the kids. The celebrations were just beginning. A 19th-century church stood on the far side of the dirt plaza. I walked over and peeked between the locked doors. As I turned, a small angry man dressed in pink pajamas strode furiously towards me, shaking his shaman's stick in my face. In his drunken slur of Huichol and Spanish, the only words I could understand were that he was going to tie me up.

"Hey Mommy, come watch," said Dashiel. "They're going to tie Daddy up."

This was not turning into the Educational Experience I had planned. There are many taboos during festivals—just taking a pencil out to jot down a note is reason enough to land a person in jail—but I hadn't expected to be bound up. The great thing about Mexico is that you can buy your way out of most situations. In this case, the price was a gallon of tequila.

The next morning I entered the village alone. About thirty cows, bulls, and sheep were tethered to stakes in the plaza. One by one, each animal met the same fate, their blood given as sacrifice to the gods in exchange for rain and abundance. With so much death hanging in the air, combined with the cheap alcohol everybody was drinking, it became a little tense hanging out in the village. Some of the Huichol made me a target, throwing prayer sticks at me as if they were darts. Later, one of the executioners held a freshly slaughtered sacrifice up to my face while lecturing me in Huichol. I hadn't a clue what he was saying, but I could imagine: *"You're next."*

The third day, all of us entered the town, Boojum trotting alongside. Things weren't going as we had planned. There had to be a way to stem this undercurrent of hostility. A group of shamans were gathered around a bonfire, drinking tequila and talking with their followers. The shamans wore round woven hats edged with long turkey feathers that fluttered in the wind. This caught Boojum's attention, as she cocked her head, ears perked. Instinct was kicking in.

"Heel, Boojum," I commanded, just as a tremendous blast of wind hit us. One of the hats gusted off the head of a shaman and hurtled through the air. Boojum paused, tail up, her body lowered into a crouch. Then she bolted.

"Boojum, heel," I screamed. "Heel goddamit," but there was no stopping her. She was running with the wind, chasing after what looked like a Frisbee with feathers. The hat was rolling on its rim when she caught up to it. Boojum grabbed it in one graceful swoop, then trotted back to me swinging the hat back and forth in playful victory while I stood frozen in horror. I took it out of her mouth, hoping that she wasn't about to start playing her second favorite game, tug-of-war.

This is her moment, I thought. Her last moment.

I gave the hat back to the shaman, apologizing profusely for the sacrilege. I recognized him as the one in the *caliguey* when we first arrived. He took the hat without saying a word while looking at Boojum in a curious way.

"Is this the dog that found the antler?" he asked.

I assured him that she was.

"She must be Huichol," he said, breaking out into a laugh. All the others in the group began to laugh as well while Boojum sat on her hindquarters, tail thumping the ground, a lopsided grin on her face. All the tension of the past two days seemed to vanish as they talked of what a beautiful dog she was. No, we couldn't sell her, we said. She was family. The conversation shifted to the ceremonies that would take place that night, which they invited us to attend. After all, Boojum had became an honorary Huichol, and we, her guests.

That night, we huddled in a smoky hut, watching the shamans eat their peyote and sip clear tequila, their dark eyes burning inward. One threw his head back as if in a trance, then began to sing the ancient songs that would last all night long. Boojum lay curled at the entrance oblivious to it all, tired after a day of working like a dog.

Facing page: *After a long walk, a golden catches her breath on a park bench. Photograph © Sharon Eide/Elizabeth Flynn*
Overleaf: *A three-month-old pup chomp-chomps on a bulbous cucumber. Photograph © William H. Mullins*

Homecomings

by Arthur Vanderbilt

One of the principal reasons to have a golden retriever in your life is to *guarantee* that no matter how obnoxious or mean your behavior, no matter the length of time you are gone, no matter how long it's been since you last bathed, there will be a golden retriever, with enthusiasm bordering on desperation, waiting at the screen door to welcome you home. For the golden retriever, the bond with people runs deep, to the depth of his soul.

Arthur Vanderbilt has seen just such a furry face waiting at the door for more than half of his life. A lawyer by training, he is the author of several books on the law and law school. But he has also written four books that had little, if anything, to do with the American justice system, including *Treasure Wreck: The Fortunes and Fate of the Pirate Ship Whydah* (1986), *Fortune's Children: The Fall of the House of Vanderbilt* (1989), and *The Making of a Bestseller: From Author to Reader* (1999).

"Homecomings" first appeared in Vanderbilt's elegant book, *Golden Days: Memories of a Golden Retriever* (1998).

A golden waiting patiently in the sunshine. Photograph © Henry H. Holdsworth/Wild by Nature

It's July. The first weekend in July. The time, 11:30 A.M. The last leg of a long trip on a hot summer Saturday morning. My sister has flown in from Washington, D.C. I arrive from Newark. We meet downstairs at the baggage area of the Delta terminal, take the bus around and around Logan to the Hertz lot, find our car, throw our bags in the back seat, and join the weekend traffic heading out to the Cape.

The noonday heat rises off the highway ahead of us, forming mirage puddles that evaporate as we reach them. The traffic is moving along. Then it slows for no reason. Now, inexplicably, it stops. We don't move twenty feet in fifteen minutes. It starts up again unexpectedly. And, of course, when we finally see the Sagamore Bridge we're moving stop and start, bumper to bumper. Crossing the Cape Cod Canal, we shut off the air-conditioner and open the windows to inhale the scent of scrub pine and saltwater that to us signifies the beginning of summer. We count off the exits along the Mid-Cape Highway that appear and disappear in tedious slow motion. Finally, at Exit 11, we pull off and continue along Bay Road, noting the new construction since Thanksgiving and then, ahead of us, the expanse of Pleasant Bay, with wind surfers darting across the water and, farther out, white sails slipping by the islands.

As we drive by the golf course, past panoramic views out over the Bay and islands all the way to the outerbeach, we unbuckle our seat belts, getting ready to get out of the car the second we roll into the driveway and come to a stop. For we know that there, looking out through the front screen door, will be a golden retriever who will instantly know that the two missing members of her pack are home.

She's up on her hind legs, pawing and pawing at the screen, barking frantically. Heeding her alert, another pack member opens the screen door and out she explodes, jumping onto us, snuggling her face against us, squeezing tight in delight, from one to the other, then racing in circles around us, with happy squealings and squeakings, a bark of joy right in the face as we kneel down to say hello, and then we're shepherded into the house straight to our bedrooms.

We place our suitcases on the floor and unzip them as Amy pokes her nose in mine, shuffling through the neat stacks of underwear and socks, pushing aside the shirts, searching.

"What do you want, Amy? Where is it? This? Oh, here it is!"

I dig in to the exact spot and pull out the new tennis ball with the delicious rubbery smell. She snatches it and races out of the room, tearing around the house with the ball in her mouth, whining and whimpering, blowing out through her nose in excitement, looking, looking, trying to locate the perfect hiding spot.

Behind the curtain? No, too obvious.

Under the chair? No good, they're all watching.

What to do? She lies down and gets in a few good chews, then at once is up again, ball in mouth, trotting over to lead us outside along the sandy path down the bluff to the beach to survey her domain.

She stops at the end of the path so that we can take it all in. The southwest breeze blowing through the beach grass. Summer smells of hot sand and cool saltwater and of the green salt marsh over on Strong Island. Down the Bay, Little Sipson and Big Sipson Islands, and behind them in Little Bay, Hog Island, Sampson Island, Pochet Island, and

A girl and her eight golden pups fit into her little red wagon with room to spare. Photograph © Jerry Irwin

Barley Neck. Beyond, the rolling dunes of the outerbeach. Above, the summer sky.

A dash to the water's edge. A look back at us: *Do you want to go swimming? No? Not now? Okay.* Back up to the house she races, checking to make sure we're right behind her. Straight to the kitchen to her water dish. She drinks and drinks, then rushes to join us in the sunroom, sitting down in the middle of the room and breathing an immense sigh of contentment.

Then and only then can we say hello to our parents.

"You know, she's been waiting patiently by the door all morning."

We get caught up on the news. Amy observes the conversation, her eyes moving from speaker to speaker, until all the really interesting gossip has been told and the talk gets boring and repetitive, at which point she lies down, her paws casually crossed, and closes her eyes. Every now and then she looks over to make sure we're still there, makes eye contact and thumps her tail up and down against the floor: *One,* bang! *Two,* bang! *Three,* bang! *Four,* bang! *Oh yes, they're all here.*

For the rest of the afternoon, she follows us around, stealing glances at us with that they're-really-actually-finally-here look. At dinner, she assumes her usual place, seated right between my sister and me with her head resting first on my sister's lap, then on mine, then back again, every once in a while smacking her nose into our stomachs to make sure her secret code still works. It does; against all parental edicts, after each smack a tasty morsel of flounder or clump of macaroni and cheese mysteriously finds its way from our plates into her mouth; and later, for dessert, a container of yogurt (lemon is our favorite) is shared, pretty much fifty-fifty. (When no one is looking, we together eat carrot strips, one starting at one end, the other at the other.)

And in the middle of the night in my dreams I hear a soft swishing and feel a presence, and opening one eye, see her head resting on the mattress a few inches from my face, staring at me. Seeing me open an eye, she swats her tail back and forth into the bed in greeting, her body wiggling in happiness.

"Hello, Amy," I whisper, patting her. Satisfied that I'm okay, she's immediately on her way to the next bedroom for a bed check, coming back once or twice more during the night to make sure, really sure, we're still there.

The first summer, when she was just a pup, when she had first checked on me in the night, I assumed she had to go outside.

"Amy want to go out?"

She looked at me, quizzically. *What the heck is his problem?*

"Amy? Okay, Amy go out?"

Well, okay, if he has to, but this is really weird. It's pitch black and scary out there and morning has got to be a long way off and I've got to make my rounds and get back to bed.

We'd creep through the house with a flashlight, out the side door, crossing the patio and the wet grass to the top of the bluff.

The Bay was making its liquid sounds. Far off, we could hear the surf breaking up and down the outerbeach and sometimes the hollow crash of an immense breaker. Starlight that had started toward us a million years before reached us at last that night. Looking out from the bluff at the Milky Way extending horizon to horizon, filling the vast night sky, it felt as if we were alone together in interplanetary space, as if the earth were moving in space and time, an island adrift in a sea of stars, and that if we didn't hold on, we would fall off.

"Here. Amy go here," I'd say, pointing the flashlight's beam on a nice spot in the poverty grass on the crest of the bluff.

What the . . . ?

"Okay, here. Amy: Amy go here."

No dice. She stares at me.

"Okay, but I'm telling you, this is your last chance, okay? I'm not coming out here again, okay? You understand that, right? This is it."

No.

"No?"

No.

"Okay. Last chance. Here, okay?" I say, flashing the light around the grass. "Amy go here."

No.

"No?"

No.

By then, we had both scared ourselves with thoughts of what might be lurking at that time of night out in the dark behind the bayberry thickets: coyotes? bears? drug-runners? kidnappers? I scooped Amy up onto my shoulder and hurried back to the house, locking the door behind us.

We both go back to bed. Several hours later I again feel the presence, the swish of a tail, the eager eyes.

Belle

by Colleen Needles and Kit Carlson

It's 5 A.M., time to do the chores. Dave Zimmerman and his golden retriever Belle roll out quickly. Dave rolls literally—a paraplegic, he's been in a wheelchair since his motorcycle was hit by a car in 1986. Belle is Dave's service dog. As his hired hand, she helps him keep the farm working, rain or shine. After breakfast, Belle brings Dave his shoes, opens the door and closes it behind them, then hops into the cab of an ATV with him and heads for the hog shed half a mile down the road.

There, Belle helps Dave clean the pig pens by bringing him scrapers and the hose, and opening and closing the shed doors. If Dave drops his tools, or needs something fetched, Belle's got it. For a reward, she gets to play with her tennis ball—when Dave tosses it, Belle races after it so fast that she tumbles head over heels to stop when she catches up. An independent, self-directed worker, Belle dislikes wearing her harness, preferring to roam and play freely when Dave doesn't need her help. Still, she'll do almost anything he asks, although she's not wild about riding on the bumpy snowplow or tractor.

Belle is a great American farm dog, but she became one only because in 1994 Dave entered a "Great American Farm Dog" contest. Sponsored by *Successful Farming* magazine and Rhone Poulenc Herbicide, the competition promised a dog to anyone who could best explain why his or her farm needed one.

Dave wrote a lengthy description of his accident, his disability, his life as the owner of a small family farm in Minnesota, and how a dog could help him carry on. Of the 429 entries the magazine received, Dave's was the most compelling.

Belle was his grand prize, selected and trained by Independence Dogs in Pennsylvania to be a service dog. The agency had never trained a dog for farmwork before, so there were lots of phone calls to the Zimmermans as Belle began to learn the tasks she would have to perform. She even spent time at the University of Delaware's swine farm to get used to working with hogs.

Finally, almost two years after Dave wrote his essay, Belle arrived. She fit right in with Dave, with his wife and two kids, with his brothers and parents (who own neighboring farms), even with the hogs. Her upbeat yet mellow personality makes her welcome wherever Dave goes, whether it's to his part-time desk job in a neighboring town, or to Walt Disney World for a family vacation. "After my accident, I was taught to do everything for myself," says Dave, "so it took me a while to integrate her into my life while still maximizing my ability to be independent. But she's made my life so much easier, so much more fulfilling."

Colleen Needles, a Minneapolis-based television journalist, and Kit Carlson, a science and nature writer, are the authors of Working Dogs: Tales from Animal Planets K-9 to 5 World *(2000), from which this excerpt is taken.*

Above: *The gentle, compliant nature of the golden and the breed's willingness to do anything for their owners makes golden retrievers ideal service dogs. Photograph © Keith Baum/Baums Away!*

Overleaf: *A helpful golden leads a horse back to stable. Photograph © Alan and Sandy Carey*

A fresh coat of fire-engine-red paint spruces up this golden's home, and she seems very happy with her new digs. Photograph © Alan and Sandy Carey

"See, Amy? I told you. You have to go out. And this time, you're going to do something, okay?"

And out we'd go and back we'd come, no farther ahead.

After several nights of this, a glimmer of slow-witted human comprehension: Amy didn't want to go outside. In fact, she has extraordinary bladder control. Rather, she was making her nightly bed checks.

Several times a night, from bedroom to bedroom she goes on her rounds to make sure everyone is all right. As long as we say hello or give her a pat, off she goes, satisfied that all is well. But if we're sleeping soundly, out like a log, she'll make her soft whining noises or bat her tail against the bed or rest her head on the mattress, staring at us until we awaken. If, perchance, a bedroom door is closed and her little noises fail to draw a response, she'll stand next to the door and wag her tail so that on each sweep it slams against the door. And if we're really out cold and that too fails to do the trick, she'll lie down outside the door, stretched right against it; and just like Atticus Finch watching over Jem at the end of *To Kill a Mockingbird,* she'll be there all night, and she'll be there when we open our doors in the morning, thumping her tail and making her morning sounds of greeting.

Up from her bed in my parents' bedroom, out into the hall, through the dark living room and kitchen she makes her way each night for her nightly head counts, down the back hall to my sister's bedroom. A quick check. Into my room. All is well. Everyone is in. All present and accounted for. Everything is as it should be. And so, back to her bed and to sleep.

Like a card counter in a casino, she always, constantly, in the back of her mind is counting who is there and who is missing; and if the numbers don't add up to four, she senses that something is wrong and worries. She's like Nana, the nursery watchdog in *Peter Pan* who tended the Darling children, Wendy, John, and Michael. Watching over us is pretty much a full-time job for Amy, what with the vigils at the front door, the bed checks, the worrying.

She's considered herself in charge right from the afternoon my parents picked her up to bring home. Breeders recommend weeks twelve to sixteen as the best time to take a puppy home for the easiest transition. Due to travel circumstances, Amy was only eight weeks old when she began living with my parents. Either she assumed from the outset that she is human, or they did a pretty good imitation of being golden retrievers; they did know how to pass themselves off as such. From the moment she swaggered into their house, like Caesar on a triumphal march surveying his latest conquest (although, unlike Caesar, her bravery always seems like someone whistling in the dark; and if something is a little frightening, she'll beat a hasty retreat to the safety of the nearest legs), she assumed her rightful position as pack leader.

It's a ragtag pack if ever there was one: a retired couple and two middle-aged children who come for visits (usually only when the Cape's weather is good), but she makes the most of what she has. The same dog who opens presents with all the enthusiasm of a four-year-old seems to sense with a philosopher's wisdom that "Old Time is still a-flying"; she considers the return of any pack member who has been away from the house for an hour or more grounds for an effusive reunion; a return after a more lengthy absence warrants a full-blown homecoming celebration.

Overleaf: *Roly-poly and a with a glimmer of mischief in his eye, a white golden puppy poses senior-portrait-like on a split-rail fence. Photograph © Sharon Eide/Elizabeth Flynn*